STUDIES OF THE MODERN CORPORATION

HERMAN W. BEVIS, CPA

Corporate Financial Reporting
in a Competitive Economy

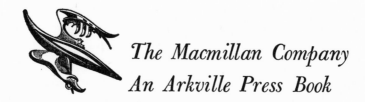

The Macmillan Company
An Arkville Press Book

THE MACMILLAN COMPANY, New York
COLLIER-MACMILLAN LIMITED, London

DEDICATED TO THE MEMORY OF

George O. May

MENTOR

STUDIES OF THE MODERN CORPORATION

Columbia University Graduate School of Business

The program for Studies of the Modern Corporation is devoted to the advancement and dissemination of knowledge about the corporation. Its publications are designed to stimulate inquiry, research, criticism, and reflection. They fall into four categories: works by outstanding businessmen, scholars, and professional men from a variety of backgrounds and academic disciplines; prize-winning doctoral dissertations relating to the corporation; edited selections of business literature; and business classics that merit republication. The studies are supported by outside grants from private business, professional, and philanthropic institutions interested in the program's objectives.

Richard Eells
EDITOR

Acknowledgments

This book probably would not have been written had not my thoughts been turned in the direction of the broader implications of corporate financial reporting by the penetrating, stimulating questions and observations of George O. May. For this reason, this book is dedicated to his memory.

My thanks go to the large number of my partners who have contributed constructive thought, suggestions, and criticisms. Not all would agree with every position taken in the book, of course, and I would not wish it otherwise. Vigorous interplay of different minds is healthy. But in both endorsement and criticism, my partners have helped.

Professor Richard Eells of Columbia University and Professor Gerhard G. Mueller of the University of Washington have provided wise counsel and stimulating ideas. I thank them. My appreciation goes also to my secretary, Miss Jean Oves, for her patient and careful work with the manuscript, which must at times have seemed to her interminable.

HERMAN W. BEVIS

Contents

Introduction

This book is dedicated to the propositions that a high standard of corporate financial accounting and reporting is as much a safeguard of the health of corporations in general as of stockholders in general; that confidence in the corporation is engendered by full and fair disclosure; and that this confidence could be shattered, with serious consequences to the freedom of corporations to operate, by any widespread deliberate suppression of information about the corporation which is needed by stockholders. United States publicly owned corporations as a group are world leaders in the disclosure of information to their stockholders. With relatively few exceptions (which prove the rule) they have the confidence of our society. The relationship is not accidental.

Corporate financial accounting and reporting has evolved from, and responded to, the social and economic environment. It is practical—designed to be useful. Yet there runs through most of it a logic distilled from sound business practices and healthy corporation-stockholder-society relationships. Corporate financial accounting and reporting today is good, but not perfect. Changes are taking place to which it must adapt. Improvements in it will come principally from perceptive analysis of the nature and activities of the corporation, its interaction with its environment, and the informational needs of investors. From such studies, sound accounting theory and logic will be equally clear.

1

Scope of the Book

This book is concerned with the financial accounting and reporting of publicly owned corporations to their stockholders. As such, it is deliberately restricted to only a portion of the whole accounting and reporting area. In addressing itself to publicly owned corporations, it does not purport to deal with proprietorships, partnerships, and nonprofit organizations, nor with closely held and owner-managed corporations. Reporting to stockholders is to be distinguished from reporting to creditors, regulatory authorities, taxation authorities, or any other group whose interests or informational needs differ to any extent from those of stockholders. The financial accounting and reporting that suits the requirements of all these others may be largely—but not necessarily entirely—the same as that most suitable for reporting by the publicly owned corporation to its stockholders. The very important field of internal reporting to management is also not intended to be covered specifically in the book. Naturally, management informational needs are more detailed than those of stockholders, but here again, many of the foundations for the two types of reports are the same.

Financial reporting to stockholders by publicly owned corporations should be examined as a field in itself. The subject is complex enough—and important enough. Of the more than one million incorporated companies in the United States, the securities of some 26,000 are quoted and have some degree of trading. Approximately 6,000 have 300 shareholders or more and comprise the bulk of the trading in the over-the-counter markets or on the stock exchanges. Of these, about 2,500 are listed on the recognized exchanges, somewhat over half being on the New York Stock Exchange. Included within the scope of the book are most of the giant American companies engaged in national as well as international business and whose names are bywords in business and financial circles and whose operations have tremendous impact on the society as well as on the economy.

To provide a foundation for occasional quantitative references, an Appendix at the end of the book summarizes totals on the recent financial statements of 100 of the 500 largest United States industrial corporations listed by *Fortune*. The $63 billion of assets of just these 100 corporations is no small accumulation of resources.

The number of stockholders of corporations is important and increasing. According to the 1962 Census of Shareowners, provided by the New York Stock Exchange, share ownership in the United States has dramatically increased since 1952. At that time, an estimated 6.5 million Americans owned shares in the nation's publicly owned companies. By early 1962 that figure had grown to 17 million. Now there are about 18 million persons in the United States who hold shares directly or through investment-trust media. The investment trusts, developed over recent decades, now have nearly $30 billion worth of securities and are owned by small shareholders the length and breadth of the land. Common stocks have become increasingly significant in the portfolios of insurance companies, pension funds, educational, religious, and charitable institutions, and in the portfolios managed by the trust departments of banks. Thus, the number of persons indirectly affected by shareholdings of institutions in which they have an interest, when added to the number of direct stockholders, becomes a sizable portion of our entire society.

On the New York Stock Exchange at a recent date, there were nine billion shares listed, and they represented, at market quotations, approximately $500 billion. Such an amount is nearly incomprehensible, but it amply indicates the need for a careful survey of the financial reporting of the corporations falling within the scope of this book.

Definition of a Corporate Financial Report

The most important external communication resulting from corporate financial accounting and reporting is the annual report to stockholders. Invariably included in these reports is a set of conventional financial statements: balance sheet or statement of financial position, income statement, and statement showing changes in retained earnings. Most, but not all, of the important financial information about the corporation is compressed into these statements and the footnotes directly accompanying them. Elsewhere in the annual report will be found—in quantitative terms and in commentary—information that is either supplementary to, or explanatory of, the data in the usual financial statement form. All of this information, wherever found in the annual report, is included in the phrase "corporate financial reporting" as used in this book, for it is to the annual report as a whole that one must look for the discharge of management's responsibility to report to its stockholders.[1]

Most of the discussion of financial accounting and reporting here will be recognized as being also applicable to corporate prospectuses. That prospectuses are not referred to is, again, merely to keep the discussion within manageable bounds.

It is said that there is a sizable number of investors who make investment decisions on the basis of only one statistic about a corporation: its net income per share or, perhaps more specifically, the price-earnings ratio. Such persons will receive with dismay the suggestion that even the entire set of conventional financial statements with their footnotes does not exhaust the historical

---

1. Some of the commentary in annual reports deals with forecasts, plans, and other projections into the future. These are *not* to be confused with financial accounting and reporting, which is essentially historical in nature.

financial information in the annual report which is pertinent to their buy/sell/hold decisions. This book will have justified itself if it does nothing more than convince a few such people that it is utterly impossible to wrap up adequately and accurately the yearly progress of a complex corporate enterprise in the single statistic of net income per share. There must be a qualitative evaluation of this quantitative statistic. Historical information for this purpose will be found in the financial statements, the footnotes, and elsewhere in the annual report to stockholders.

I

Reporting to Society

Corporate directors and managements have a key role in economic affairs. Their responsibilities are heavy and their authority broad. They render an accounting for the results of their actions. The corporate financial report, nominally addressed to shareholders, also maintains a healthy corporation-society relationship. Corporate profit is the strong connecting element. The principle of full and fair disclosure underlying the corporate financial report is deeply imbedded in both corporate and social thinking.

W henever a continuing mission of importance requires the assignment of responsibility and delegation of authority among people, the relationship usually also involves a periodic accounting of the uses of these responsibilities and powers. Society has, in general, assigned to corporate directors and management the responsibility of employing resources gainfully; after delegating commensurate discretionary authority over the utilization of capital, society expects, and receives, the accounting to which it is entitled.

Some students of the corporation look at the role of the accounting discipline in society in terms of ethical relationships. They point out that corporations, like other organizations of humans, contain powerful built-in forces for disintegration as well as for progress and stability. One of the keys to the successful governing of organizations is the ability to sense these potential weaknesses and root them out. As human organizations and in-

7

stitutions grow larger and more complex, they can become prey for self-seeking men. The less their accountability, the easier it is for them to misuse their power and to violate the fiduciary relationship assigned to them by the "owners."

The growth of the large corporation, however, has been accompanied by the development of a remarkable system of accounting and accountability. Its apparent objective has been to measure profitability and to indicate performance, efficiency, and growth. It is not at all farfetched to add that simultaneously we have been developing a powerful instrument of discipline, not only for the modern corporation, but for large segments of Western society as well. For when a man is obliged to make financial accountings of his activities, the discipline becomes more or less a part of his character and imposes on him much higher ethical standards measured in terms of social responsibility than if there were no reckoning. The highest ethical attainment is reached when a man accepts this accountability as a challenge to measure himself by his willingness to report fully on the results of his own actions. Looked at in this way, a practical observer of the corporate scene can agree with the academicians that the accounting discipline works hand in hand with rising ethical standards of the society.

Taken literally, what are corporate financial reports—the end products of today's concept of corporate accountability? They are communications from specific people to specific people. Originating these communications are identifiable members of the management and the board of directors. Receiving them are equally identifiable people—those on the stockholder list at the cutoff date for mailing the report. The fact that these reports sooner or later may be received by thousands of other persons should not obscure the fact that they are essentially communications rendering accountings to present stockholders from the stewards of their resources. Moreover, the fact that prospective

investors may use the information contained in the report to
assist them in making projections in connection with investment
decisions does not belie the report's essential nature and purpose
as an historical accounting of what has taken place.

The foregoing assessment of the place of the financial report
in the corporation-stockholder relationship suggests that it is a
semiprivate communication or, at least, that interest in it is nar-
rowly confined to those who are, or who would be, investors. But
this is not so. Concern about the welfare and progress of our
large corporate enterprises clearly transcends that portion of the
society made up of stockholders. Interest in corporate financial
reports involves much more than mere curiosity on the part of
outsiders. Whether the corporation makes profits or suffers losses,
especially over a period of years, is an indicator of the potential
security or stability of employees, sometimes of entire communities, of creditors, competitors, suppliers, customers, and governmental revenues from taxation. Take all corporations together
and the interest and concern of society are widespread and obvious. It is this fact that suggests that the responsibility-authority-
accountability chain of the corporation and its management be
examined more closely.

CORPORATE RESPONSIBILITY

A society such as ours which endorses free and competitive
enterprise is not articulate in assigning specific responsibilities
to its various component parts for accomplishing economic, social,
political, and technological progress. One does not find laws delegating particular tasks to particular corporations, for example,
to create resources, to innovate, develop, manufacture, distribute,
or educate as to need and use. Therefore, to assess positively
what roles have been assigned by society to corporations, one
must search for responsibilities that evolved with the institutional

development of corporations and that society does not prohibit even though it has the power to do so.

Students of the corporation are stressing the widening range of its responsibilities in matters political, sociological, international, and cultural. Consider, for example, this statement by Eells and Walton:

> If we concede that there is an accountability that goes with wealth and power, then the logic of responsibility for those who hold it is easy to establish. The corporation is a center of wealth and power, and it has, therefore, responsibilities to those most dependent upon it. These are its stockholders, its employees, and its customers. But its employees, its customers, and its stockholders are also the community. Therefore, it has a social as well as an economic responsibility.
>
> To assess the nature of this responsibility is one of the functions of management. It is a difficult assignment, one that requires imaginative thought and sensitivity to future trends. Two things we can be reasonably sure of: this is not a static age, and the modern corporation is not a static institution. Nor are the responsibilities of the corporation unalterable. The obligations of the large business enterprise have already altered so much that they bear little resemblance to those of the individual entrepreneur of the earlier free enterprise economy. Gradually, business has taken on the characteristics and the responsibilities of all comprehensive institutions. As a result, there has been a strong tendency to move away from the older concept of the business firm as having primary responsibility to its owners toward the concept of the firm as a multifunctional institution with diffused responsibilities.[1]

However, a book on corporate financial reporting must confine itself to those responsibilities of corporations which are economic. These alone are awesome. Corporations are responsible for searching out and developing a large part of the nation's natural resources and for directing enormous capital and effort to manufacturing, transportation, communication, and distribution activities. Much of the responsibility and credit for technological and other innovation rests with them. The budgets of the federal

---

1. Richard Eells and Clarence Walton, *Conceptual Foundations of Business* (Homewood, Ill.: Richard D. Irwin, Inc., 1961), pp 458-459.

government and many state and local governments rely heavily on tax revenues from them.

Documentation of the importance of the role of the corporation in the nation's economic status and progress is so extensive in current literature that it seems unnecessary to summarize it here. There is general agreement that the responsibilities are enormous. Furthermore, it can be argued that society has *assigned* these responsibilities to corporations by not exercising its power to restrain the scope and volume of their economic activities.

AUTHORITY RESTING WITH THE CORPORATION

In a system of competitive enterprise the degree of freedom that corporate officers and directors have to manage the resources at their disposal is the best index of the authority that they exercise. Conversely, any external curb upon the freedom to operate might be regarded as a negation of that authority, or some part of it.

The management of any so-called "unregulated" corporation can enumerate many restrictions upon its freedom to make economic decisions. Take, for example, the following areas: antitrust; bargaining with organized labor; conservation of natural resources; social security; health and safety; minimum wages; and fair trade practices. An abnormally high corporate income tax can also be a widely applicable and effective restriction on the ability of the corporation to grow from within by plowing back its resources.[2]

---

2. An interesting rediscovery of both the corporation's role in economic growth and the stifling effect thereon of high income tax rates appeared in 1962-64 when additional allowable depreciation deductions, investment tax credits, and reductions in corporate tax rates were instituted by the federal government for the avowed purpose of stimulating growth. Not the least of the possible reasons for this change in government taxation policy was that the nation, caught in a race with Russia for economic growth, turned to the corporation for the desired impetus.

Notwithstanding these and other limitations on the authority of corporate directors and managements, it is clear that executives still retain wide discretionary authority over managing a significant portion of the resources and capabilities in the nation.

If it might be said that authority without responsibility is anarchy, and that responsibility without authority is stupidity, so responsibility and authority without accountability is dictatorship. That our corporations are not so cast is evident from the fact that they are required to, and do, render accountings which, although addressed to stockholders, also serve the purposes of society at large.

CORPORATE PROFITS: CONNECTING LINK BETWEEN
SOCIAL AND STOCKHOLDER INTERESTS

The wider social interest and that of the stockholder in the corporate financial report come squarely together in looking to see whether a corporation made a profit or suffered a loss. Reference was made earlier to the number of important groups to which this is an index of potential stability or instability. But the social interest in a corporation's profits goes beyond the mere negative fear that lack of profits indicates the corporation's potential demise. The interest is also positive; it desires that the corporation create more wealth than the resources of labor and materials it consumes in the process. Subject only to the imperfections inherent in translating "wealth" and "resources" into the common denominator of the monetary unit, it must be concluded that society, like the stockholder, must hope that the corporation makes a profit.

That the two interests harmonize can be illustrated by listing the principle steps involved in the operating cycle of a corporation and expressing their significance in both socioeconomic and financial terms, thus:

Socioeconomic

1. The corporation draws down from the remainder of society some of the latter's human and material resources.

2. Some of the resources are converted into productive facilities and equipment (still a resource, usable by others in society if not by the corporation itself; resources have not been "consumed").

3. Other of the resources are expended in the form of research and development. At the time of the expenditure, there is no assurance in most cases that a useful product or service will emerge, or at least that the new resources created will be equal to those consumed.

4. Still other of the resources, and some of the usable capacity of the productive facilities and equipment, are converted into physical products or services to be turned over to society, with a reasonable expectation that society will value the product at least at the equivalent of the resources of labor and materials directly consumed in production.

5. Some of the resources of labor and materials are expended in promotion, selling, and general and administrative functions of the corporation. Society sees no *direct* relationship between these activities and the resources that are being or will be turned over to it by the corporation. Therefore, society considers the

Financial

1. The corporation makes a cash disbursement, or obligates itself to pay cash later, for labor, materials, services, and facilities.

2. The corporation records the substitution of one asset for another; e.g., fixed assets for cash. The corporation has not yet incurred an operating expense.

3. The corporation at the time of disbursement does not know whether a salable product or service will emerge, or whether what emerges can be sold at a price to recover all costs. In most cases, it does not "capitalize R&D"—which would substitute an intangible asset for cash. The corporation considers that it has incurred an operating expense.

4. The corporation considers that the production process adds value to the raw materials processed and, again, substitutes the asset of inventories for the cash disbursed for labor and materials and for the fixed assets consumed.

5. The corporation, too, does not consider that expenditures for these functions can be directly related to products or services being produced, or that the value added can be demonstrated. Therefore, it records the expenditures as expenses at the time they are made. (There are some exceptions in special cases.)

Socioeconomic (cont'd)	*Financial (cont'd)*

Socioeconomic (cont'd)
resources consumed at the time the labor and materials are utilized.

6. The remainder of society receives a resource from the corporation in the form of a product or service. The value placed upon it is represented by a monetary price determined in the market place. This price may be more or less than the monetary equivalent of the resources used directly and indirectly in putting the product or service into the hands of society. Usually, the price is more, indicating that society considers the corporation to have discharged its responsibility successfully.

Financial (cont'd)

6. The corporation records revenue from sales. From this revenue it deducts all costs directly associated with the products or services sold. Other expenses are attributed to the period in which the sale took place. The result is reported as net income or net loss. Usually it is a net income, the magnitude of which, in relation to capital employed, indicates the degree of financial success of the corporation.

The foregoing brief analysis contains two important matters of timing—one having to do with revenues, the other involving expenses. The corporation does not ordinarily record revenue at the time of development of the product or, for that matter, at the time when the product has been successfully produced. The corporation must first find a consumer for the product and persuade him to buy it. From the socioeconomic standpoint, it is only after both development of a useful product *and* its acquisition by a consumer that anyone external to the corporation (society) receives anything of value from the process. Neither purpose—that of society or that of the corporation—would be well served if the corporation reported that it had created more resources than it had consumed, if by valuing the product and putting it on the shelf at its expected sales price, it then learned that it could not find a buyer to consume it.

The timing of the recognition of costs and expenses, as opposed to the conversion of assets from one form to another as operations proceed, is also significant. The controlling philosophy

is essentially a prudent one, namely, that resources or assets have
been consumed unless they can be directly related to a resource
or asset regarding which there is a reasonable expectation that
the costs can be recovered through future revenues. Harmony is
preserved between the social and financial viewpoints of the
corporation by this approach. There would be disharmony, for
example, if the corporation reported its consumption of resources
in research and development as a mere conversion into another
asset form (in accounting language, if it capitalized R&D expenses) but did not develop a product.

If, then, society looks to corporations to accomplish the same
general objectives that the stockholders set for them, it is not
accidental that corporate financial reports to stockholders also
adequately discharge the corporations' accountability requirement to society. It is also not accidental that the principle of full
and fair disclosure has become deeply imbedded in our system.

Recognition of Full and Fair Disclosure

The principle of full and fair disclosure of corporate financial
affairs has been in evidence from the early days of widespread
ownership of corporations. It is true that early recognition was
spotty, confined to progressive managements, bankers, and audi-
tors who recognized that stewards should make an accounting
to other people for the use of their money. The principle is still
not fully embraced by some parties involved; however, today
these must be considered exceptions so sufficiently few as to emphasize the enormous progress made in past decades.

One group, external to the corporation but constantly studying and promoting disclosure from the last century to the present,
has been the independent accountants. Before and after the turn
of the century, they borrowed freely from the experience and
practices of England, then a large supplier of capital to the

United States. Independent accountants have long since oriented themselves to the specific conditions in the United States, and remain in the forefront in studying and promoting improved disclosure. They do this as individuals and firms and through their national professional organization, the American Institute of Certified Public Accountants.

The New York Stock Exchange—the earliest and still the most prominent United States securities market—commenced its pressures for disclosure by its listed corporations before the turn of the century. The first step was a *recommendation* in 1895:

> This Exchange recommends to the various corporations whose securities are here dealt in, that they shall print, publish and distribute to stockholders, at least fifteen days prior to annual meetings, a full report of their operations during the preceding fiscal year; together with complete and detailed statements of all income and expenditures, and a balance sheet showing their financial condition at the close of the given period. And this Exchange urges the stockholders of the several corporations to take such action as may be necessary for the accomplishment of this recommendation.[3]

The next step was a listing *requirement* in 1899:

> Original applications to list any securities of Industrial or Manufacturing Companies must be accompanied by . . . [an] agreement that the Company will publish at least once in each year a properly detailed statement of its income and expenditures for such preceding period, and also a Balance Sheet, giving a detailed and accurate statement of the condition of the company at the close of its last fiscal year or of recent date.[4]

The Exchange recalled many years later that:

> The demand of the investing public for publicity in corporate affairs was not a sufficient force at that time to make effective the request of the Stock Exchange and it was some time before such an agreement was obtained from substantially all listed companies.[5]

---

3. Committee on Stock List, New York Stock Exchange, March 1, 1895.
4. *Ibid.*, March 22, 1899.
5. New York Stock Exchange, *Bulletin*, August 1939.

Throughout the era of corporate growth until the thirties, the standards set by nongovernmental parties for financial disclosure ran far ahead of those established by law (with some exceptions for regulated industries, where accounting and rate-making were closely allied). State incorporation laws practically ignored the form and content of disclosures to stockholders. State "blue sky" securities laws dealt to some extent with disclosures in connection with the sale of securities, but specific requirements dealt with minimum rather than the best prevailing standards.

The federal government dramatically entered the field of corporate financial reporting for nonregulated companies with the Securities Act of 1933 and the Securities Exchange Act of 1934. The description of the former, immediately after the title, commences: "An act to provide full and fair disclosure . . ." Minimum standards of disclosure of financial data set by the Securities and Exchange Commission initially and to date have been high but reasonable. They apply both to prospectuses covering public sales of securities and to annual reports required to be filed with the commission.

Amendments to the Securities Acts in 1964 extended the commission's jurisdiction to many companies with widespread stock ownership not listed on a stock exchange. Also in 1964 the commission, by issuance of a regulation, took some cognizance of financial reports sent directly by companies to stockholders. The new rule requires notation and reconciliation in stockholder reports of those accounting-principle differences from reports to the SEC that have a material effect on financial position or results of operations. The rule permits suitable condensation or omission of details, provided such procedure does not result in the omission of "any material information necessary to a fair presentation or to make the financial statements not misleading in the circumstances."

Thus the principle of full and fair disclosure to stockholders—

long recognized by progressive managements, investment bankers, and independent accountants—has become public policy in the United States as formally reflected in federal laws, rules, and regulations. The same is true in England, Canada, and Australia (as evidenced by their Companies Acts), as well as in some other countries with important or increasing degrees of industrialization.

Notwithstanding the minimum standards set by the federal government and the stock exchanges, the broader responsibility for decisions as to disclosure and other aspects of the financial reports continues to rest with corporate directors and managements. A recent study of the reports to stockholders of 100 of the larger industrial companies in the United States strongly suggests a voluntary trend toward more and more disclosure. Presumably, the specific additional items of disclosed information have been chosen by each company with the objective of more clearly presenting its particular situation.

This suggests that most managements and directors at least accept seriously the accountability phase of their stewardship, or that they clearly recognize in self-interest that full and fair disclosure passes part of the responsibility for assessing the corporation's status and progress from them to the users of financial reports. There is undoubtedly another force behind the trend. Large corporations not only compete with one another in the capital markets but each strives to obtain its capital as cheaply as possible. Information about the company is one of the conditions being imposed more and more by the sophisticated suppliers of capital or their advisers. Institutional investors and the analysts of financial houses, specifically, are contributing to the pressures.

The harsh light of full disclosure does not make all companies look equally good or equally promising, of course. Those whose story is sad do not relish the telling. That they usually do tell their stories, however, is of great significance in our economic and social system. This country derives a tremendous thrust to economic progress from the use by its corporations of great accumulations of capital in productive endeavors not feasible for smaller units. The willingness of the multitude of distant investors to supply the capital must rest to a large extent on their confidence that, when the corporate financial report arrives, it will contain a full and fair presentation of the financial position of the corporation and the results of its operations—good or bad. Individual cases have shown time and time again that, if investor confidence is shaken in *this* respect, then confidence in management and the board of directors is shaken in *all* respects. The importance of the corporate financial report must loom large, therefore, not only in corporation-stockholder relations, but also in corporation-society relations.

Summary

A high quality of corporate financial reporting may be looked upon as a manifestation of, and an inspiration to, higher ethics in our society. It may be viewed as the accounting which society receives for the responsibility and authority lodged for productive use of a significant portion of the nation's resources. It may be thought of in its literal sense as a report to stockholders from their stewards. In any one, or all, of these senses, its implications and potential deserve thoughtful consideration.

II

Roots of Financial Accounting and Reporting

The roots of financial accounting and reporting lie in the nature of the corporation and in its interplay with the environment. Therefore, the corporation must be studied and explained before its accounting can be understood. The large, publicly owned corporation normally has broad-based operations, undertakes risks of large magnitude, often for very long terms, and evolves and changes in response to its environment. It is continually facing and attempting to assess contingencies of the future. All of these facets have profound implications for corporate financial accounting and reporting. They are its roots.

The fact that any corporation's financial report is strongly oriented to the nature, position, and activities of the corporation cannot be surprising; the report *is* the corporation insofar as financial data can depict it. The corporation and its reactions to environmental forces are dynamic rather than static; so also must be its financial accounting and reporting.

To the extent that generalizations are, or are not, valid as to conditions, operations, and transactions of all corporations, so also they may, or may not, be valid as to the accounting and reporting of all corporations. That these generalizations are relatively few is understandable in view of the large number of widely ranging variables that apply to the circumstances of individual corporations. Those few widely applicable conditions and propositions are dealt with in this chapter.

PERTINENT LEGAL FOUNDATIONS

The corporation is a creature of the law. Any consideration of legal theories and technical applications of corporation laws is beyond the scope of this book and, in any case, must be left to students of the law. However, a layman can readily recognize that there are three provisions of corporate laws without which the large corporation could not exist, namely: limitation on liability of stockholders; grants of long life; and the authority to own property.

The possibility that an action might give rise to liability of undeterminable amount is a strong deterrent to taking that action. Certainly this would be true of a person contemplating investment in a corporation if his personal fortune were to be at stake should the corporation need it to discharge its obligations. Laws that specifically limit the extent to which the corporation may legally call upon the stockholders' resources remove this obstacle. The rights of stockholders to participate in the affairs of the corporation are also limited—essentially to the right to vote for directors and to vote on propositions, such as plans for mergers and acquisitions, increases in authorized stock, stock options, and liquidation. Thus, the distinction between the corporation and its stockholders is clearly drawn in both directions.

The life granted to corporations by their charters, if not perpetual, usually spans several generations of men. As limited terms near their end, charter renewals are easily obtained. This feature is essential to the modern corporation's activities. Consider how few and limited would be corporate activities if chartered lives ran for only, say, ten years and renewals were uncertain. The right of the corporation to own property, similarly taken for granted, is naturally also a necessity.

From these key legal foundations, we may turn to some of the economic characteristics of the corporation which have an important bearing on its financial accounting and reporting.

The Interrelationship of Risks, Internal Dynamics, and External Stability

There is a limit to the financial risks which any entity can run. The objective is success in the long run, but when it is reasonable to expect that some ventures will *not* be successful, or will be unsuccessful for an interval or so of time, caution must be exercised against overoptimism. Moreover, the willingness to undertake risks is affected by the prospect that reasonable stability in environmental conditions will or will not exist until the ventures involved are brought to a conclusion.

RISKS

Modern corporations are engaged daily in making risk-taking decisions. The decisions have to do with whether or not the commitment of sums of money gives reasonable prospect of advancing the corporation to a better position than if the sums were not expended.

Many of the issues involved are less than dramatic and would be characteristic also of smaller businesses: to replace the roof or a truck, or to repair it; to add the new salesman, or to pass up the potential additional sales; to buy common stocks, or to buy bonds. Many decisions to spend money do not anticipate a tangible gain but, rather, an intangible one: corporate donations, an employee recreation area, an institutional advertisement.

But the risks which characterize the large, publicly owned corporation and which also give rise to the most important problems of accounting are the big ones—particularly the big ones with the long "payout." Long-lived factories, buildings, machinery, transportation and communication facilities, and other such physical assets will come to mind immediately. So too will large-scale and long-range programs for research, explorations for new mineral deposits, huge advertising and promotion campaigns, or large investments abroad. Perhaps not so easily visualized as a risk-taking commitment, recoverable only if future revenues prove it to have been justified, is the building up of an effective team of *people*, with the attendant recruiting and training costs in time and money.

Many corporate programs like the foregoing are the better because they are larger. Efficiencies, economies, depth or breadth of programs could not be realized on smaller scales. The advantages of mass production and mass distribution have been well publicized. However, there are advantages deriving from size in many other directions—ability to finance to best advantage, for example. From whatever reason, the large size of commitments to the future is an important characteristic of the corporation.

Long duration of the commitments is another characteristic. Few multimillion-dollar projects are initiated, developed, and brought to a conclusion within the course of a year. On the contrary, projects and programs that must span 10, 20, 30 years or more to achieve optimum success predominate. Most would be considered failures if they did not run a good part of their initially projected span. Be it the utility plant, the pipeline, or the people and facilities in a distribution system or a research effort, the risk is that the fruits of the present commitment will not be realized before the program's course is run, and the attraction is that it will run its course and make a profit.

The size and length of the corporation's commitments-at-risk, made possible by corporate law, are an overriding influence on corporate accounting.

INTERNAL DYNAMICS

The spreading of risks is more characteristic of the larger corporations. Whether it be in investing abroad, maintaining lines of products, reliance on customers, or in any other area, the corporation tends to diversify risk. There are exceptions, of course. But, generally speaking, corporations have attracted or internally generated sufficient amounts of capital to enable them to diversify. An important corporate urge since before the turn of the century, in fact, has been in this direction. Moreover, reassessment of risks and profit-making opportunities is continually taking place.

The large corporation may appear to the casual observer to be engaging year in and year out in repetitive activities of the same type. It is true that the results of these activities will usually dominate the corporate financial report. However, a look beneath the surface will show that changes in some portion of the corporation's business activities—each taken alone having the appearance of being unusual or nonrecurring—are continually taking place. Abandonment of major product lines and their related plants and facilities to concentrate on more profitable business is not uncommon, nor is the abandonment of high-cost plants while opening lower-cost ones. Some major business investments may be liquidated while others are being initiated. Reflection will suggest that such actions are necessary if the corporation is to be successful within a changing environment.

The fluidity of the corporation through liquidating some of its activities while initiating others has, in fact, resulted in a remarkable record of survival for the whole. A compilation by the First National City Bank (New York) showed that, of the 100 largest manufacturing corporations in 1919, only one had actually gone into liquidation by 1963, although a number of the others had lost their corporate identities through mergers.[1] Al-

---

1. First National City Bank (New York), *Monthly Economic Letter*, August 1964.

though some might say that mergers are tantamount to liquidation, or that the latter would have been inevitable had not the merger opportunity arisen, this is not the explanation in most cases. True, the merged companies' activities may have been gradually made over, so that in 1963 they bore little resemblance to those of 1919, but this occurred for continuing corporations also.

In summary, whereas it is the law that creates an opportunity for the corporation to have indefinitely long life, it is the continuing adaptation of the corporation to a changing environment that effects the realization. Past economic experience lays the foundation for an assumption as to the future, namely, that the corporation will *continue* to have indefinitely long life. Such an assumption is implicit in the policies and decisions of many varied groups. Directors and managements cannot but endorse this assumption when they commit huge resources to investments, research and development, loans, and fixed assets which cannot both "pay out" and yield a return on investment over other than a long, long period of time. Investors who pay prices for corporation stocks which are equivalent to 10, 20, or 30 times a corporation's earnings at the current rate must, consciously or subconsciously, be making the assumption. Employees plan their entire careers around a corporation, with no assumption other than that it will last indefinitely. Finances of the federal government rely heavily on the yield from corporate income taxes; although this is no indication of an assumption with respect to the life of any particular corporation, collectively it implies an important assumption as to both life and profitability.

Stability in Public Policy

The undertaking of large, long-term risks by the corporation must, of necessity, be accompanied by the assumption that there will be no major change in those conditions that are vital to its survival, if not its success. The corporation is geared to accept changes in the forces of competition, in technology, in markets, even a certain degree of rise and fall in general economic activity. It considers these normal hazards; they are challenges that sharpen the faculties. But the corporation is totally unprepared for any major change in the substantive rules of the game by the government under which it operates.

For example, continuance of the respect for the private property rights involved in the long-term commitments is a *sine qua non* for the corporation. The international corporation sees this clearly. Confiscation (the ultimate in disrespect for such rights) in any one country sends a shudder throughout the corporate world, and may put the confiscating country on the international corporate black list for decades. Expropriation with inadequate payment is little better. The commitment for the long-term payout inherent in modern industrialization and the short-run risk of confiscation of property are not compatible.

In matters other than property rights, the corporation, to make its economic contribution, also requires stability in public policy. The usurpation by government of any decisions normally reserved to the corporation in a free-enterprise system will introduce uncertainty; for example, President Kennedy's entrance into the steel price action in 1962. Any government that introduces laws discriminating among corporations, such as whether they are foreign or domestically owned, will create a degree of instability. So will changes in laws to handicap some corporations while benefiting others, or measures that interfere with the investment or repatriation of capital across national lines.

One of the problems facing international corporations is instability in international exchange rates, including the freedom, or lack of it, to convert one currency into another. Maintaining a stability in these matters, so that the international corporation can operate successfully, goes well beyond a government's political attitude. It extends to fundamental forces of inter-

f

national finance and trade over which the government has only partial control. Some international corporations, while adjusting to the prevailing instability as best they can, are evincing increasing interest in helping to find solutions to the overall balance-of-payments problems of countries in which they operate. Their self-interest in the success, if not the survival, of their business in the country is thus broadened into an interest in the integrity of that country's currency in international circles.

The influence of the corporation toward stability in environmental conditions important to it may become even more widespread. Although the corporation may well turn away from the *initial* commitment where present or prospective instability is serious, once it is committed it can be counted on to use all the power and influence at its command in the direction of stability. Again, the size and length of term of its commitments impels it to do this, thus making it one of the strong stabilizing forces in a society. World War II was followed by an upsurge of nationalism in many countries. But accompanying this phenomenon was an equal if not greater desire for industrialization and improvement in standards of living. As a result, the expansion of corporate activities across national borders has been unprecedented. Undoubtedly, in most countries the desire for the higher standard of living will outweigh the impeding nationalist sentiment, to the end that the international corporation will be allowed more and more to make its contribution. If this is so, the international corporation will probably find itself wielding greater and greater influence in world stability—financial, economic, and even political.

Stability in Economic Conditions

Although the corporation must enjoy stability in governmental policy in those areas vital to its existence, the corporation does not necessarily require that the general economic activity of its environment proceed on an even keel. In fact, the corporation has geared itself to weather economic storms. One of its strengths is its very ability to to sustain itself through adversity, while smaller and weaker economic units fail under depressed conditions. Corporations watch economic trends and forecasts closely and are continually on the alert for forthcoming dips, as well as rises, in general business conditions.

Whether corporations must evaluate their risks in terms of survival through another depression as severe as that of the 1930's evokes different opinions. Most, it would seem, think not. Certainly, in the United States, the policy enunciated in the Employment Act of 1946 and its subsequent implementation place the federal government's resources and influence squarely behind relative economic stability. The purpose of that act (Public Law 304—79th Congress) was stated to be: "To declare a national policy on employment, production, and purchasing power, and for other purposes." One of the duties and functions of the Council of Economic Advisers, created by the act, is:

> To develop and recommend to the President national economic policies to foster and promote free competitive enterprise, *to avoid economic fluctuations or to diminish the effects thereof,* and to maintain employment, production, and purchasing power. (Italics added.)

The first annual report of the council to the President contained this statement in the last paragraph:

> Wise policy and action on the part of labor, of management, of agriculture, and of finance, with a very carefully considered complementary role by the Government, will not only raise the national prosperity to new high levels *but will maintain those levels with a degree of stability which has not characterized the earlier exploratory and speculative decades of our industrial life.* (Italics added.)

There may be little new in the foregoing philosophy, but it seems clear that the postwar period has seen a more intense interest in economic stability than in any previous period in United States history. More exchanges of views have taken place within the private sector, and there have been more formal and informal pressures from the federal government to keep within bounds the factors that make for economic fluctuations.

If the corporation watches the general economy, the latter also watches the corporation. For example, one of the important national economic indicators is the amount of corporate profits (and the dividends therefrom). Fluctuations in this particular index have important implications both for the private sector and with respect to the government's revenues from taxation; they also have a psychological effect on the economic mood of the nation. There is no doubt that, given a free choice between steadiness and fluctuation in the trend of aggregate corporate profits, the economic well-being of the nation would be better served by the former. Thus, in laying the groundwork for later examination of corporate financial accounting and reporting, it is pertinent to observe here that society will welcome any contribution that the accounting discipline can make to the avoidance of artificial fluctuations in reported yearly net incomes of corporations. Conversely, the creation by accounting of artificial fluctuations will be open to criticism.

Implications for Financial Accounting and Reporting

The foregoing analysis of the nature of the corporation and its interplay with the environment establishes many of the major characteristics of, and challenges to, corporate financial accounting and reporting. The interrelationship of corporate nature and activities with corporate accounting and reporting may be diagrammed thus:

From:	*Derives:*
Large and long-term commitments. The indefinitely long life of the corporation. The admonition to avoid artificial distortions in reported periodic net income.	The accrual basis of accounting.
Diversity of activities and risks.	Variations in accounting for investments.
Uncertainties as to the future.	The identification of contingencies.
Changes in corporate programs.	Unusual gains and losses.

The Accrual Basis of Accounting

There are two extremes in systems that could be used to account for receipts and expenditures that enter into the computation of the periodic net income of a corporation.

The cash basis: This method treats every cash receipt and expenditure as revenue or expense in the period in which the transaction takes place. If large amounts are sporadically involved—in receipts, say, on long-term construction contracts or installment sales, or in disbursements for supplies or a build-up of inventories—it is obvious that net income from year to year will fluctuate widely. A new or expanding business would show huge losses in earlier years, followed by large profits later.

The accrual basis: This method has as its central objective the transferring or apportioning of the financial effect of transactions and events from the period in which they occur to the period or periods to which they may appropriately be related. It attempts to match revenues with related costs where a physical relationship is identifiable and to establish a logical, systematic, and objective method of apportionment where the direct connection cannot be established.

Large corporations universally use the accrual basis of accounting as their basic method. The many questions and problems involved in its application are dealt with later, including occasional accounting treatments under the accrual basis which closely resemble the cash basis. However, it may be noted here that in the use of the accrual basis of accounting in general, and almost always in decisions thereunder in accounting for particular types of items, the effect is to minimize distortions of net income which could be attributable to accounting method as opposed to actual transactions and events.

The accrual basis of accounting would be indefensible for the large, publicly owned corporation were it not for the assumption that the corporation is to have indefinitely long life. As mentioned earlier, it is a common characteristic of such corporations that they are able to, and do, expend large sums on facilities, investments, and other items which can be recouped from revenues only over a long period of time. Some of the fixed assets, particularly, have an expected useful life running into three or four decades or more. The carrying forward of these expenditures as "assets" in the balance sheet at more than their salvage value would be out of the question if the life of the corporation were assumed to be only a few years. The assumption of indefinitely long life for the corporation, however, makes this permissible.

This assumption of longevity cannot be applied blindly. The appearance and disappearance of smaller corporations each year remind us that the assumption is always subject to re-examination in any company, large or small, when signs appear that point to impending liquidation. Wherever portions of a business within the corporation are being "phased out," a realistic case in liquidation accounting is presented; the burden is strong to scale down or eliminate from the balance sheet those "assets" which in these circumstances become known or reasonably anticipated losses, as well as to provide currently for any future losses arising from existing commitments that must be liquidated.

Whether and when to abandon the assumption of indefinitely long life for the corporation *as a whole* is an extremely difficult matter for judgment. What implications as to corporate life, for example, should be drawn for those railroads with a consistent period of losses and a bleak economic outlook? Are the un-amortized historical costs of their fixed assets appropriately carried forward as a charge against future revenues under the accrual basis of accounting? Actually, corporations involving a strong public interest, like the railroads, can go through more than one reorganization or quasi-reorganization without endangering the assumption of indefinitely long life for their *operations*. Even corporations that are dispensable from society's standpoint are more likely to lose only their identities through mergers than to discontinue their operations abruptly through liquidation.

The assumption of indefinitely long life for the corporation under the accrual basis of accounting is useful because of its general validity in economic experience. Implicit in the assumption, also, is that the corporation will, on balance, make a profit —that it will achieve the objective for which it was organized. This, too, is demonstrated by experience. The assumption is more than that it will merely break even over the future. For corporations that experience a series of losses without reasonable prospects of reversing the trend, generalized assumptions (which are the foundations for the accrual basis of accounting) cannot be made; they are outside a pattern. Whether from the standpoint of the creditor, the stockholder, or the accountant, each such corporation is a case to be studied and dealt with by itself. In general, the practice is not to disturb the amortized historical cost of properties, inventories, and other such "assets" until a reorganization or quasi-reorganization takes place.

These are some exceptions that challenge the tenets of the accrual basis of accounting. However, under more typical corporate conditions, business operations are continuous; research, plans, and programs extend over several years, if not decades. Expenditures and revenues involved in these can be directly associated with the entire number of years which a program spans, although a given portion of the total cannot be associated directly with any one year within the life cycle. Corporate reported net income for short periods of time should not be distorted solely by the accounting method chosen for reflecting the financial consequences of these events and transactions. This is the basic mission of the accrual basis of accounting.

ACCOUNTING FOR INVESTMENTS

Usually the large corporation is engaged in a variety of programs or ventures that are wholly or partially separable from one another. Some are being commenced while others are nearing a conclusion. The objective of each venture is usually to make a profit and (for the American corporation) this means in the long-term view a profit realizable in dollars. But there are risks and uncertainties between the making of the commitment and that ultimate realization. The venture may not be profitable at all. Or it may be profitable as a self-contained unit, but obstacles may arise to the realization of its profits by the owning entity.

How should separable investments and ventures be reported to the stockholders? Should the current net income of the separable activities be reported as a part of the overall net income or not? Which activities should be considered an integral part of the "enterprise" and which treated as separable "investments" by that enterprise?

In answering these questions, judgments and estimates as to risks and stability are necessarily involved. The treatment in one case may be inappropriate in another. For example, portions of a corporation's business may be in separable risk ventures, each with limited life expectancy. Like trading ventures in the early days of the sailing ships, these can be viewed differently, depending upon their number, variety, and their pattern of overall success. Contrasts are presented today, for example, between the "one-shot" drilling syndicates and the far-flung oil producing companies, or between the corporation formed to produce one play or one motion picture and those that embrace such ventures by the score.

The range of treatments of investments in corporate financial reports, with particular reference to the underlying earnings, is set out below. The investments involved may be in incorporated or unincorporated businesses, domestic or foreign.

Cost recovery accounting for an investment: The cost recovery approach dictates that income be applied to reduce the investment until it is recovered or at least reduced to a minimum salvage value. Those using this method assess the risks and uncertainties of the future so high that they are unwilling to admit the first dollar of profit until they are made whole in their own currency on the investment.

The future proves them right if aggregate income never exceeds the investment, for it is then seen that it would have been misleading to have recorded and reported the amounts received as current income. The future proves them to have been in error in reporting periodic income if ultimate income exceeds the investment. It can then be seen that all the income is bunched up in the later periods, whereas it was actually earned more evenly over the entire term of the investment.

The cost recovery approach can well be the most appropriate accounting when risk is concentrated and its degree is high.

Reporting of cash receipts as income: A middle ground in accounting for the results of operations underlying an investment is provided when income therefrom is reported to stockholders only to the extent received in the currency of the parent. This approach suggests a reasonable expectation that risks and uncertainties do not endanger ultimate recovery of the original capital invested.

On the other hand it suggests unwillingness to equate, say, current earnings abroad, which are reinvested there instead of being remitted, with other earnings currently being reported to stockholders. Whether this is excessive conservatism or laudable restraint—or even whether the cost recovery approach should have been taken toward the earnings that *were* remitted—is a fine matter for judgment as to reasonable expectations in the future.

Reporting all current net income: The greatest degree of confidence in the future of the separable operation is exhibited, of course, by the reporting of full current income earned by it on the same basis as if the income had been earned by the parent company itself, and without regard to the portion currently remitted to the parent.

In this connection, the accounting for investments abroad is again an interesting illustration. Full reporting of earnings with respect to a foreign country can be justified by one company, when it might be questionable for another operating in that same country. Diversification of risk among many countries, for example, permits taking the setback here and there, without serious distortion of overall reported results; a company not so well diversified may need to be more conservative in reporting its foreign earnings.

The more technical aspects of combining separate entities to present the consolidated financial position and results of operations of the enterprise will be discussed later. However, an important consideration in applying the technique will be assessments of the degree of risk and of future stability in the underlying operations.

CONTINGENCIES

The foregoing touches mostly on accounting for income from separable activities, or "investments." In addition to the risks and uncertainties to be evaluated there, other uncertainties frequently must be noted in corporate financial reports in a category that might be called "contingencies." This covers questions known to exist, but resolution lies in the future, or the ultimate financial impact is uncertain. In this context a contingency is regarded as any possible future event the financial effect of which is not reasonably determinable, whether the ultimate result presently appears favorable or unfavorable. Unresolved claims asserted by or against the corporation, tax controversies, and unrealized appreciation are illustrations of contingencies.

Contingencies can be reduced by judgment and estimate to dollar amounts and then entered among the assets, liabilities, revenues, or expenses of a set of financial statements. Recording the estimate does not make the contingencies disappear, however; it merely formalizes a current appraisal of them. Only the future can prove whether the step should or should not have been taken. In other words, a contingency exists until facts and events resolve it; accounting techniques cannot eliminate it.

UNUSUAL GAINS AND LOSSES

It has been observed that the accrual basis of accounting attempts to avoid distortions of net income by reallocating receipts and expenditures affecting net income from the periods in which they occur to those to which they more rationally apply. If each component of the corporation proceeded on a steady and unwavering course to its predetermined objective, the accrual basis would yield periodic net incomes affected by little other than economic trends. This is usually what happens in the case of the mass of transactions and events affecting the corporation.

However, we have also noted the dynamics that are characteristic of most corporations. Plans and programs are changed; supposedly permanent investments are disposed of; plants, products, or product lines are discontinued before their costs are fully recovered. Many of these changes may be said to be abrupt, and unless they occur with frequency or are relatively inconsequential, the gains or losses from liquidating the efforts must be considered unusual. They are "distortions" in the financial results of the corporation's operations which, in most cases, judgment and estimate applied under the accrual basis of accounting could not anticipate and prevent.

For many corporations, it is infrequency and size in relation to a single year's operations which render the items unusual in relation to repetitive activities. Looked at over a large number of years, the items are less unusual and more clearly a phenomenon associated with the corporation's adaptation to changed conditions. In any event, a fair treatment of unusual charges and credits is another challenge for corporate financial reporting and will be taken up later.

Stability of the Monetary Unit

When aspects of external stability important to the corporation were examined earlier in this chapter, stability of the monetary unit was not included. Stability of foreign currencies has been touched upon, but not the stability of the currency of the parent company's own country; the latter is discussed here.

It is both a blessing and a curse that a wide variety of corporate facts, transactions, events, and estimates are reduced to the so-called "common denominator" of one currency in the process of financial accounting and reporting. The blessing is that, otherwise, the heterogeneity involved would not lend itself to comprehensible summarization and communication. The curse is that the purchasing-power equivalent of the monetary unit does not always remain stable—sometimes, or in some countries, not even reasonably so. The 1945 and 1965 dollar may appear to be equivalents, but the meat and potatoes that the former bought are greater than the latter. The same is true of 1963 Brazilian cruzeiros and those of only *one* year later. Under these circumstances, how does the corporation best compute resources that it has created in comparison with the resources that it has consumed in the process?

Particularly in the English-speaking countries, the assumption has been widespread in society that the purchasing power of the monetary unit will remain *relatively* stable. Life insurance is underwritten in huge amounts even though the monetary units paid today will be returned, with only reasonably low interest, decades hence. In these countries debt maturing many years later is placed at interest rates that are sharply lower than those for six- to twelve-month loans in countries where the assumption is rather that the purchasing power of the monetary unit may decline sharply.

Concern about inflation has been virtually universal in the period since World War II. In many countries, the problem has been to cope with radical inflation as a fact. In others, including the United States, the United Kingdom, Canada, and Australia, the problem has been rather how to contain inflation within reasonable bounds. Of interest statistically is that in these latter countries it has become common practice to correct many important economic monetary indices so that they are expressed in "constant" monetary units, i.e., with an attempt to remove the effect of changes in purchasing power.

In American business, banking, and investing circles, there has been some discussion in the postwar period of the effects of inflation on the corporation. Most of the consideration of the problem has come from companies with heavy investments in long-term fixed assets, and has been oriented to the computation of taxable income. These companies have pointed out that corporate taxes, levied on a net income computed after a depreciation allowance based only on the historical cost of long-term assets, drain off corporate resources so as to make difficult the replacement of the facilities at inflated prices. Pressure on even this point subsided somewhat with the commencement of accelerated depreciation allowances and investment tax credits for tax purposes.

However, not all of the problems of inflation are resolved

when the computation of taxable income is adjusted somewhat for its effects. The measurement of corporate net income for reporting to stockholders remains in question. In measuring the periodic net income of the corporation, particularly its costs, among this year's costs may be dollars spent this year (say, for labor) and dollars spent twenty years ago (this year's depreciation of fixed assets). Should this year's cost of plant exhaustion be the historical dollar, or its present purchasing-power equivalent? What recognition should be given to loss in the purchasing power of working capital itself?

With annual increases in the price level of, say, only 1.5 to 3 per cent, many contend that such concern about the reliability of annual reported net incomes is unwarranted—that the inevitable tolerances which must be allowed for estimates and judgments are at least as great and that, therefore, penny refinements are a waste of time when dollars are the measure. However, the cumulative effect of slow inflation on invested capital is not so easily dismissed. The proposition was advanced in Chapter I that society has assigned to the corporation the responsibility of contributing to economic growth, of creating more resources than it consumes in the process of creation. To the extent that reported growth of the corporation is overstated because it is reported in dollars without measurement of their decline in value, then society, corporate management, and the stockholder are all misguided. No one is aided by such reporting.

The dollar of yesteryear is not the same as that of today. Translation of dollars of different purchasing power is required to communicate in the same language, just as translation is required from pesos to dollars. Here, the governmental, business, financial, and investing segments of the society need to be educated still further as to the lack of stability in the monetary unit and the practical consequences thereof in all economic matters (including income taxation). Large, publicly owned corporations, dealing as they do in long-term commitments, are in an excellent position to demonstrate the effects of deterioration in the purchasing power of the monetary unit and should take every opportunity to do so. Until they, and others similarly directly interested, shake the general willingness to act as though the monetary unit is stable, it will be extremely difficult to obtain acceptance of the proposition that corporate financial accounting should report periodic net income in constant dollars.

Most of this chapter has been devoted to an analysis of environmental factors to which the corporation and its financial accounting and reporting have reacted and adjusted. When it comes to decline in the purchasing power of the monetary unit, many corporations may be said to have reacted partially by hedging through borrowing long-term money. Income taxation authorities have taken some steps, such as broadening acceptance of the last-in, first-out inventory method and authorizing accelerated depreciation, which partially offset the effects of inflation. Corporate financial accounting and reporting has not made the coordinated adjustment to this environmental factor which it has made for other factors.

SUMMARY

The corporate financial report is molded to a substantial degree by the nature of the corporation and its reaction to the environment. Some generalizations about corporations have been advanced; some variables have been noted, and others will appear later. However, because the report is a communication adapted to the stockholder's needs, the stockholder also influences the nature and content of the report and its underlying measurement techniques. This subject is developed in the next chapter.

III

Stockholder Needs

Because the corporate financial report is a communication to stockholders, the nature of these stockholders and their principal informational needs are highly pertinent in shaping the communication. What
significance attaches to the growing corps of financial analysts? Since
the large, publicly owned corporation is not expected to be liquidated,
must the stockholder's primary interest center on corporate net income?
If so, what problems arise in appraising the significance of such income
for as short a period as a year, in view of the unusual transactions and
events that occur sporadically and the contingencies that are usually
present? What significance does the balance sheet have to the stockholder? What responsibility does the stockholder have not to misunder-
stand or misinterpret data furnished to him?

The corporate financial report is utilitarian in nature
and purpose. It is designed to communicate useful information.
No degree of symmetry in its artistic form, nor in the logic behind
it, justifies the report if it does not successfully communicate.
Usefulness is its supreme test. But useful to whom? What informational needs are to be met?

The short answer, of course, is that the report is addressed to
the informational needs of the stockholder. This answer may
seem so obvious as not to require the stating. However, in practice such is not always the case.

There is no question but that many nonstockholders obtain
information useful to them from the reports and will continue to

do so. However, this is not necessarily the case for all nonstock-holders. For example, a corporation's net income for the year, fairly computed for stockholder purposes, may be derived from both civilian and military business. The portion attributable to the latter is not necessarily a fair measure of the profitability of the military contracts. Research and development expenditures may quite properly have been charged to income in prior years for stockholder purposes but still be directly related to this year's sales to the military. This example illustrates a situation frequently encountered, namely, that accounting and reporting to stockholders on the enterprise *as a whole* may well require alteration in order to report fairly on *one or more of its parts*. Short-term creditors constitute another group that does not necessarily find in the stockholder report all of the information— or information in the form—that it desires. Taxation and regulatory authorities are other such groups.

Because it is known that nonstockholders use the corporate financial report for their purposes, the temptation is often great to broaden both the accounting and the reporting to accommodate the more diverse needs. To this there can be no objection as long as the primary purpose is served equally well. However, where the stockholder's needs and the other informational requirements become divergent, the stockholder's needs must take precedence.

WHO ARE THE STOCKHOLDERS?

Stockholders are highly diverse in nature: individuals, corporations, associations, and partnerships; profit-seeking and eleemosynary; domestic and foreign; insiders and outsiders; wealthy and not-so-wealthy; those investing for themselves and those investing for others. In numbers, American investors are said to be about 18 million, suggesting widespread dispersion of ownership. At the same time, nearly 20 per cent of the value of securities listed on the New York Stock Exchange is said to be held by "institutions" (insurance companies, funds, and trusts), suggesting concentration of ownership. Diversity, then, rather than similarity, describes the stockholder. Both the dispersion and the concentration, however, have implications for corporate financial accounting and reporting.

Corporation shares numbered in the millions change hands daily. On the New York Stock Exchange alone, four- to six-million-share days are the rule. A large industry is devoted to making it easy to buy and sell securities. The members of the New York Stock Exchange, the underwriting houses, and the over-the-counter houses, who may not be members of the New York Stock Exchange but who are members of the National Association of Security Dealers, maintain a network of offices (numbering several thousands) catering to all the cities of the country. This system is tied together by a communications network that permits transactions and information to move with electronic speed. An order to purchase or sell securities from any part of the country can be consummated in a matter of minutes.

The Securities and Exchange Commission, an agency of the federal government of the United States, maintains a nationwide surveillance of exchanges and the transactions executed on them. Security issues that must be registered with the SEC cannot, in general, be offered without full disclosure of information concerning the nature of the company, its financial position, and the financial relationship of interested principals. The overall purpose is to maintain honest dealings, free of manipulation, to prevent fraud, and to assure the fairness of the information presented by the corporation to the public. Speculative risk and judgment as to the success of the corporation remain with the individual.

Both the elaborate arrangements to assure the far-flung stockholders' liquidity in their investments and the public interest in the machinery emphasize one thing: many stockholders of today can—and do—sell tomorow, their places taken by others who will, in due course, also sell. Among the millions of stockholders, then, there are many whose relationship with the corporation will shortly be terminated. At the same time, there are many others standing by who may at any time enter into a stockholder relationship with the corporation.

The ephemeral stockholder is in sharp contrast to the indefinitely long life of the corporation and the long span of many of its programs. It is out of this relationship of the permanent to the impermanent that an important reason for the periodic corporate financial report arises. A person considering buying or selling shares needs information to make an investment decision; the large number of persons who at any one time have this consideration in mind emphasizes the need for full and fair information about the corporation as currently and as continuously as is possible.

This book concentrates on the *annual* financial report as the most important single financial communication from the corporation to its stockholders. However, several other important communications will be found: press releases of spot news; special letters to stockholders; proxy statements; informal releases through data in quarterly and semiannual statements.

The limitations of interim financial statements must be constantly borne in mind. A high degree of estimate and judgment must necessarily enter into the measurement of a corporation's net income for even as short a period as one year. This applies even more to semiannual and quarterly periods. At the same time, it should be observed that sales data for short periods are reliable for most corporations, and that costs may also be reliable for those corporations whose operations are characterized by simplicity and evenness.

Another aspect of the dispersion of corporate ownership

which has significance for financial reporting is the rise of the financial analyst. One may hardly expect that many among 18 million people would have the time, aptitude, or competence to make the best choice among potential investments. They need advice. Investment advisers are available to them locally or through mail services. These men vary in their competence, of course, but all purport to be more sophisticated than the "man in the street." Acting as investment advisers themselves, or backing up others in this function, are financial analysts.

INSTITUTIONAL INVESTORS AND FINANCIAL ANALYSTS

As has been said, an estimated one-fifth of the value of shares listed on the New York Stock Exchange is owned by institutions. The proportion is expected to grow to nearly one-third before long. This trend is perhaps the most important development of the last two or three decades in terms of significance to corporate financial reporting. Such institutions demand, and can digest, more information than most investors. Their investment committees are backed up by full-time financial analysts. The latter, together with the analysts in security houses and advisory services, are growing in number and importance.

It is currently reported that there are more than 8,000 financial analysts. This field of activity, which began early in the century in the larger insurance companies and trust departments of banks, has emerged over the last 30 years with a public identity. Many institutions of higher learning in the United States have established graduate schools of business that give master's and doctor's degrees in the several aspects of business administration, including financial analysis. Now a growing corps of university-trained personnel regularly interviews the managements of the corporate enterprises of the United States in which there is any sizable degree of public interest. The result is widespread dissemination of description, commentary, and analysis, as well as criticism, of the progress and prospects of these companies.

The emergence of the financial analyst, and the growing importance of the institutions he represents, have the following implications for corporate financial reporting:

1. Financial analysts are increasingly sophisticated readers of financial reports. Their abilities must be taken into account when the report is prepared. The report cannot be prepared with only the lay reader in mind.

2. Financial analysts are asking for more information about companies than has been universally disclosed in the past. Many of their institutions do, or have the potential to, influence investments to such an extent that many managements will accede to their requests. Some institutional investors, with such large holdings that liquidation would seriously depress market prices, may feel "locked in" to the point where they have to interest themselves much more directly in corporate affairs and developments than the classical idea of the ephemeral investor would suggest.

3. Corporate managements who disclose information to a few inquiring analysts will tend to make similar disclosure to all stockholders, so as not to run the risks attaching to selective disclosure.

In looking for the characteristics of the stockholder to whose informational needs the financial report is addressed, there seems no question, then, but that the institutional investor will be the most exacting; what is full and fair disclosure to him should be adequate for any other stockholder. In fact, the problem in the future will become how to avoid overcomplicating the report to the point that comprehension by the less sophisticated investor is reduced. This problem is discussed in Chapter VII.

The Principal Stockholder Interest:
Corporate Net Income

If itemized chronologically one by one, the millions of transactions and events to which a corporation is a party during the course of a year would comprise the most complete of all possible reports about the corporation. However, it would not be intelligible to anyone. Summarization in some logical pattern is necessary to make a comprehensible—and, therefore, useful—communication. The summarization could be carried out in more than one way. Since the report is addressed to stockholders, it is pertinent to look for their primary interest as the focal point in developing information for them.

Stockholders as a group, whether institutions or individuals, are suppliers of capital to an enterprise assumed to have an indefinitely long existence. Any gain to them, therefore, cannot be assumed to derive from the liquidation of the enterprise. This suggests, as the ultimate interest of the corporation's owners, the return on their investment in the form of cash dividends.

In these days of high income tax rates and lower capital gains rates, it may seem strange to mention cash dividends as an important stockholder interest. For example, many stockholders are known to seek investment situations in which current cash dividends are low but in which there is promise of ultimate capital gain. For some stocks, the market prices are so high in relation to the current cash dividend rate as to suggest that this is the least of the factors interesting stockholders. Moreover, large corporations as a group only pay out as dividends in the neighborhood of 50 to 60 per cent of current earnings, further suggesting that pressure for current cash dividends is not great.

However, all of these factors—again in contrast to the indefinitely long life of the corporation—are relatively short-range considerations of individual stockholders. The individual who buys a stock without regard to the cash return he personally will receive from the corporation does so in the expectation that he or his beneficiaries will later be able to resell the stock to someone else at a higher price. But the attractiveness of the stock to that future buyer or his successor in the chain of transactions must rest on ultimate dividend prospects. Taking stockholders impersonally as a group, the longevity of which equals that of the corporation, cash return on capital invested must emerge as the long-range focus of interest.

Future cash dividends of the corporation will come of course from the profitable employment of its capital. As the corporation moves along its course, its capital is successively made up of (1) that previously employed and (2) current earnings not paid out as dividends but added to existing capital. Thus, even without new financing, capital employed is steadily increased and—subject to the ability of the corporation to use the additional capital profitably—the ultimate dividend prospects are multiplied.

We start, then, with ultimate cash dividends as the long-term interest of the impersonal group of stockholders whose span is that of the corporation. When we come down to the people of today, however, *the primary interest of stockholders lies in the corporation's net income*—its "earnings," in the terminology of the financial community. Earnings become a composite index of two factors: coverage of current dividends, and extent to which resources have been increased. This conclusion that earnings are the primary focus of current stockholder interest provides a basis for shaping financial statements to best meet stockholder informational needs.

ANNUAL NET INCOME FIGURES USEFUL TO THE STOCKHOLDER

If one were forced to choose from among the financial statements that which bears most directly upon the stockholder's primary interest, it would of course be the income statement. And if one were forced to choose the most significant of all the figures thereon, it would have to be "net income for the year." However, without detracting in any way from the importance of the statement or the figure, both may reasonably be termed oversimplifications when one considers that they relate to the progress in the short period of one year of an endeavor as complex as a large corporation. The income statement and the net income statistic are like many a medicine—good for a purpose but still labeled "use with care." Notwithstanding the limitations, the fluidity among investors requires preparation of the annual income statement and the computation of the net income per share. As George O. May observed: "The reporting of business income for short-term periods would be indefensible if it were not indispensable." Corporate financial accounting must set about to meet the requirement in the best possible fashion. What approach best meets stockholder requirements?

Events and transactions that do or may ultimately enter into the computation of a corporation's net income may be classified into three groups which follow the nature of the corporation's activities as developed in Chapter II: (1) the repetitive, (2) the sporadic, and (3) the contingent.

Repetitve transactions and events account for the major dollar amounts of revenues and expenses shown in the annual income statement of most corporations. In fact, a significant part is represented by cash transactions completed during the year. These obviously require little estimate and judgment as to the amount which should enter into the year's net income computations. Closely associated with the repetitive transactions and events are the allocations to years, in a systematic and rational manner, of receipts and expenditures that can be clearly associated with the repetitive transactions and events of two or more years. Fixed assets, inventories, and prepaid expenses are some examples.

The stockholder clearly needs to know the annual financial result of the repetitive transactions and events and the systematic allocations. These are the firmest, in terms of resources consumed and created, as evidenced by dealings with parties external to the corporation. The *trend* in the net result of repetitive transactions is likely to be discernible and, therefore, of interest to the stockholder. At the same time, the stockholder must be on guard for trends in the historical data that are influenced by temporary external factors.

Sporadic events and transactions need to be differentiated from the repetitive ones *to the extent that they are unusual in financial effect.* In other words, they should be combined with the results of repetitive transactions and events only if the historical trend in the latter would not be distorted.

The sporadic items in mind here are completed transactions or events, or those sufficiently near consummation that their financial effect can reasonably be determined: the disposal of plants and investments, or the discontinuance of major product lines, for example. The corporation's resources have been, or are clearly about to be, increased or decreased as a result of these sporadic transactions or events. The stockholder needs to know this, the amount involved, and the nature of the items. Such information—still historical—may suggest to him whether or not he should anticipate similar happenings in the future.

Contingencies present by far the greatest source of uncertainty surrounding the measurement of a corporation's annual net income. The problem is whether or not to allow this measurement to be affected by contingencies and, if so, to what extent. The contingency can be in either direction—a potential gain or loss. Following are some examples:

> 1. The corporation holds an asset the market value of which is now double its cost, but the corporation has not yet sold the investment and realized the appreciation. Is the unrealized appreciation already income to the corporation? The corporation makes an important mineral discovery. The values involved will be realized by the corporation as the mineral is extracted over, say, the next 40 years. Assuming that it can be measured (more than likely it cannot with any assurance), is

the unrealized discovery value already income to the corporation? If so in either case, current income would be increased at the time the unrealized appreciation was discovered, and an asset in equivalent amount would be established in the balance sheet.

2. The corporation has invested in plant and equipment for a product line which, when these costs are only half-amortized, the corporation decides to discontinue on the grounds that it cannot any longer be produced and sold at a profit. The "phase out" will require three years, at which point there will have been realized a loss to the extent of the then-unamortized plant and equipment plus interim operating deficits. Are all the ultimate costs associated with the decision to discontinue the product line charges against the corporation's income at the time of the decision, or as events giving rise to the loss are concluded over the next three years?

3. The corporation invests in marketable securities which then decline in quoted market prices to 75 per cent of their cost. It is not known whether future changes in market prices prior to disposal will or will not offset the unrealized depreciation. Disposal is not contemplated at the present time. Is the unrealized depreciation to date a charge against the corporation's income

4. A corporation reports more income to stockholders than it computes on its federal income tax return. The tax paid is less than an amount determined by applying the tax rate to the income reported to stockholders. The difference in income is attributable to the deduction of more depreciation for tax than for stockholder purposes. Taking depreciable equipment item by item, there is an ascertainable time for each item when tax depreciation will "cross over" and become lower than that reported to stockholders. In relation to stockholder income, there will be a "pay back" of the tax in respect to the particular item. Taking depreciable items in the aggregate and with a reasonable expectation of constant replacement, however, which is in harmony with the assumption of indefinitely long life for the corporation, the repayment is deferred to a period believed to be indefinite, but reasonably projected, to be not less than 30 years hence. Is, or is not, the current deficiency in income tax payments in relation to stockholder income a contingent cost that should *currently* be charged against income reported to stockholders?

5. A corporation adopts a pension plan for its employees. The pension payable to each employee is a function of total years of service and of total compensation from the corporation during that service. At the time the plan is adopted, existing employees have accumulated service and compensation credits in varying degrees for pension pur-

poses. Actuaries estimate that, on a man-by-man basis at the time the plan is adopted, the amount required to fund these past-service credits would be, say, $50 million. At the same time, they estimate that payments for currently accruing service credits plus interest on the past-service amount would create a fund large enough to pay all maturing pensions indefinitely, *provided* the number of current employees did not decrease and the "mix remained approximately the same. Under this assumption, the $50 million would not have to be paid. If the level of employment (and of currently accruing credits) drops one-fifth, then a proportionate part of the $50 million will be needed over a period of time, and so on. However, logical projections using reasonable assumptions indicate that none of the $50 million will have to be paid in the foreseeable future, and that, taking the darkest view, no payments of it should be required earlier than 20 years hence. Considering these imponderables, is all or any part of the actuarially estimated $50 million associated with past-service credits a contingent cost that is an appropriate charge against *current* corporation income?

All of these illustrations introduce the dimension of time into the computation of net income of the corporation for the current period. How imminent, or how remote, is the completion of the event or transaction that will effect a realization of—that will reduce to fact—the income or expense? If the prospective completion is near-term, there is less likelihood that unforeseen factors will change the estimated result. If the completion is not a reasonable expectation in less than 25 years, or 50, and can be importantly affected by future developments, the outcome cannot be described with assurance. The dimension of time, then, having as it does a direct bearing upon the reasonableness with which the future may be predicted, is an important consideration in determining the income currently to be reported to stockholders.

The corporation is, of course, in the best position of all the interested parties to assess the nature and imminence of a contingency. In its resolution of those which should and should not enter into the measurement of current net income, however, it must bear in mind the stockholder's interest in that figure as an index of coverage of current dividends plus the extent to which resources have been increased. With this introduction, these brief observations may be made as to the treatment of a few types of contingencies in relation to stockholder interest:

1. If part of the resources reported in the balance sheet is represented by investments, plant, equipment, or other assets in which a loss is foreseen with some assurance, then to that extent the corporation's resources have been impaired and should be reduced. (Some exceptions will be found in regulated utilities.)

2. If events to date commit as a practical matter some of the corporation's resources to absorb a loss in the future, an amount should be set aside as a reserve or liability to absorb the loss.

3. Theoretically possible but highly speculative future calls upon the corporation's resources (for example, a *threat* of a loss in an asset which judgment deems to be temporary, or contingent liabilities deemed to be remote) do not suggest that it would be useful to set aside and earmark corporation resources to cover the contingency. The net long-term result of such a course would be to take amounts out of invested capital (through charges to current net income) and report them elsewhere in the balance sheet indefinitely. This would lack usefulness; capital actually employed indefinitely in the business would commence to be classified in the balance sheet in different places under different names.

4. Unrealized appreciation in a corporation's resources—from such sources as increase in market prices or mineral discoveries—do not increase the amount of productive resources available to the corporation until the appreciation is realized. Only then will the corporation have enlarged resources to put to other productive use. If the corporation continues to maintain and operate the appreciated asset, the enhanced value is realized in higher investment or mineral income. Similarly, the stockholders' invested capital is not increased by the occurrence of appreciation, but only by its realization through sale of the asset or the increased income from it.[1]

It is in the nature of the contingency that information about

---

1. The investment trust is an interesting exception; it reports its portfolio of securities at their market value and therefore includes unrealized appreciation when it exists. However, considering the nature of the trust's business, the exception is not startling: it is a buyer and seller of market values. The market values are readily determinable and (subject to blockage) realizable in the ordinary course of business, and its stockholder interest runs to the current market value of the portfolio as well as to the trust's income.

unrealized appreciation, depreciation, revenues, and costs, useful
to the stockholder in his appraisal of reported periodic income, is
difficult to define. Faced with imponderables involved in contingencies and knowing that realizations in some will come evenly
and gradually and in others abruptly, the stockholder is in need
of as much information about these contingencies as can be made
reliable. This applies whether or not management resolves its
dilemma by including such amounts in the financial statements.
A contingency does not disappear merely because entries concerning it are made in accounting records.

The Stockholder's Interest
in the Balance Sheet

It might appear from the foregoing discussion that the stockholder's informational needs are virtually satisfied when he is
supplied with the income statement—that he has little need for
the balance sheet. This is not the case.

One important type of information, contained exclusively in
the balance sheet and in related supplemental disclosures, has
to do with the liquidity of the corporation. The general assumption that the corporation will have indefinitely long life must be
continually tested for validity in the individual case. The prospect that the corporation will not have the liquid assets to meet
maturing obligations may not indicate the early demise of the
corporation as such, but it raises a clear question as to whether
the current stockholders' interests may soon be reduced or
eliminated in favor of creditors. Short of indicating such violent
readjustments, the balance sheet can indicate the extent to which
the credit line has been used, possibly give clues as to the need
for near-term financing, and suggest the cash capacity to pay
more, less, or the same dividends.

A second informational area of great significance to the stockholder ties in directly with his primary interest—the reported corporate income. This income is calculated without taking into account certain revenues and expenses—items which will enter the income statement eventually but which are considered not yet to have matured to the point where they affect income. These exclusions comprise such deferred credits as advance collections for services yet to be performed, and such deferred costs as inventories, fixed assets, and prepaid expenses. The amounts of these items—important in the balance sheet itself—constitute a kind of gigantic footnote to the income statement. They throw a great deal of light on the rate and extent of absorption to date of those income and expense items which are amortized over a number of accounting periods.

The modern balance sheet is discussed more extensively in later chapters, where the foregoing points are further developed. However, one segment of the balance sheet—stockholders' equity —needs to be explored now, for it has some relationship to the stockholder's interest in net income and dividends.

Significance of Stockholders' Equity

The stockholders' equity under consideration is that attaching to common stock, i.e., excluding any amounts assigned to preferred stock. The subject may be approached from the standpoint of the significance to the stockholder of the total and of its component parts.

Total equity: Some analysts make a computation, which might be called "return on invested capital," by dividing net income by the amount of stockholders' equity. For the intended purpose, no better statistics are available, and probably no better ones could be devised. However, those making the calculation should do so with eyes wide open—with full appreciation of the nature of the stockholders' equity figure. In particular, they should appreciate that it is not a current valuation. The assets of which it is a partial offset are not complete (most intangibles and discovery values are left out), and those listed are by and large at their historical cost less such amounts as have been amortized against income. Some of the historical costs may be quite old and therefore not inflated by changes in the purchasing power of the monetary unit.

The best indication of the fallibility of stockholders' equity as a useful measure of current value has been seen in attempts to use it as a measure of "excess profits" for tax or military contract renegotiation purposes. The experience here is that, time after time, the historical figure has had to be adjusted or subordinated to some other approach to arrive at an equitable measure of excess profits.

Components of stockholders' equity: The composite statement of financial position of the hundred large industrial corporations in the Appendix shows the following, exclusive of preferred stock and treasury stock:

	Millions
Stockholders' equity:	
Common stock	$10,479
Capital surplus	5,198
Retained earnings	26,581
	$42,258

The foregoing subdivisions may be described in general terms as follows:

1. *Common stock*—The par value of stock of that category or specified amounts for no-par stock either paid in by shareholders or transferred from other capital accounts primarily by stock dividends or stock splits.
2. *Capital surplus*—Amounts dedicated more or less permanently to the corporation. Includes excess of proceeds received for stock sold over par value (or specified amounts for no-par stock). Also includes

excess of amounts of retained earnings capitalized over par value (or specified amounts for no-par stock) of any shares issued in stock dividends and other voluntary transfers from retained earnings. Some corporations combine capital stock and capital surplus for financial statements. It is usually recommended that for specific corporations a more descriptive title be used for the account, e.g., "other paid-in capital" or "capital in excess of par value."

3. *Retained earnings*—Net amounts earned by the corporation since inception less dividends and amounts transferred to capital stock and capital surplus.

Only generalized statements can be made about the stockholders' equity section of corporate financial statements as a group. The equity section is affected significantly by the individual corporation laws, as well as by the provisions of the individual corporate charters which prescribe the characteristics of the specific issue.

What is the usefulness of these subdivisions of stockholders' equity in the balance sheet? The most frequent answer is that the amount of retained earnings indicates the limits to which dividends can be paid. It is also sometimes suggested that it is useful to distinguish between a corporation's dedicated capital and the retained earnings that have not been earmarked for any purpose. These answers need examination as to practical usefulness for the large, publicly owned corporation.

If society, acting through state incorporation laws, can be said to have set up one accounting requirement, it is that a distinction must be made and maintained between capital and income. The legal requirement was, and is, narrow and pointed. It is addressed to directors, admonishing them not to pay dividends out of capital, and was created primarily as a protection for creditors. It called for an accounting that would show whether or not capital would be impaired if a dividend were paid, which is another way of asking whether undistributed net income to date is sufficient to cover the dividend.

The capital referred to in the preceding paragraph is "legal

capital." Most large, publicly owned corporations have accumulated as stockholders' equity considerably more than their legal
capital. For the hundred large industrial corporations, for example, besides the $5 billion identified as capital surplus (probably
not included in legal capital), retained earnings were two-thirds
more than the total of capital stock and capital surplus. For only
one-fifth of these companies were retained earnings lower than
the total of capital stock and capital surplus.

To the extent that the large, publicly owned corporations like
these have financed their own growth internally, then, by retaining rather than distributing earnings, the significance of "retained earnings" as limiting the amount available for dividends
has lost force. In most cases, potential dividends are limited
much more by the amount of cash above minimum operating
needs and expansion requirements, if not still more by restrictions in indentures and credit agreements.[2]

Even if distinctions among types of common-stockholder
equity may have largely lost significance from the standpoint of
being the practical factor limiting dividends, it may still be
suggested that, when the currency has been relatively stable,
there is usefulness in segregating and identifying retained earnings as an index of cumulative growth from within, or of showing
stockholders both invested capital and earned but undistributed
increment. The point with regard to the individual stockholders
carries little weight, however; most of them bought into the
corporation much more recently than the time when its original
capital was paid in, and many since the last new capital flotation.
In other words, they bought their shares from other stockholders
and not directly from the corporation. They must inevitably con-

---

2. For the hundred large industrial corporations, retained earnings of $26.6
billion compared with $16 billion of net current assets and with $6 billion of
cash, marketable securities and receivables, less current liabilities. Sixty of the
companies had entered into covenants restricting the amount of dividends payable
from retained earnings, however.

sider their personal capital invested in terms of the price paid for their stock, rather than in the per-share amount of what the corporation calls capital.

Historical statistics on the cumulative amount of income earned but not distributed may well be useful to financial analysts and economists as indices of past growth, conservatism in paying dividends, and, accordingly, financing from within. For many companies, however, such statistics are no longer pure: portions of retained earnings have been capitalized in connection with stock distributions to stockholders, acquisitions and mergers for stock, and the like. The significance of amounts of reported retained earnings has been impaired accordingly.

In summing up consideration of the corporation's obedience to the admonition that it maintain a distinction between capital and income, these conclusions seem warranted: (1) corporations often impound and identify as permanent capital more than the minimum legal capital; (2) what accountants call capital (the sum of amounts for capital stock and capital surplus) still falls short—usually, far short—of the corporation's capital indefinitely invested in the business; and (3) if the reported amount of accumulated retained income is inaccurate, it is on the side of understatement because additional amounts often have been reclassified as capital which actually have been earned and retained by the corporation.

What does this mean to the stockholder? It adds up to, in essence, the practical concept that the entire common-stockholders' equity is the corporation's "capital." Distinctions among "capital stock," "capital surplus," and "retained earnings" are not, for most large corporations, useful to anybody. A corporation's "capital," then, increases—not spasmodically as it occasionally sells a new stock issue—but more gradually. In short, the "capital" of most corporations must be considered to include their retained earnings.

Would it, then, be less confusing and therefore more useful if financial reports showed only one figure for the total of all types of common-stockholders' equity? For nine out of ten of the hundred large industrial corporations, the answer would be in the affirmative; the amount of retained earnings of each was more than five times the current year's dividends, so that potential dividends out of accumulated earnings were more effectively limited by other factors such as available cash. The other companies were in a less comfortable retained-earnings position and, therefore, reporting separately their relatively low retained-earnings position might be important. However, half of these companies reported parenthetically or by footnote that they had covenants restricting the payment of dividends to even less than the amount of reported retained earnings. A strong case for reporting the amount of retained earnings as a potential dividend-limiting factor exists only for the remainder.

It is believed that most businessmen, bankers, economists, and knowledgeable investors would concur in the view that large corporations' retained earnings must be considered an integral part of invested capital. It is probable that they have held this view for some decades. Accounting thought has reshaped more slowly.

Consideration of the significance of distinctions between capital and income may be concluded by observing that corporate experience has outmoded what both the law and accounting term "capital." Neither's term is sufficiently encompassing. The entire stockholders' equity in the balance sheet could, from the standpoint of describing the facts of corporate life, be appropriately described by some such term as "invested capital." Moreover, for most corporations, subdivisions of the amount among "capital," "capital surplus," and "retained earnings" would appear not to convey particularly useful information. The presentation is positively misleading to anyone who looks upon a large amount of retained earnings as measuring a "kitty" which could be split up at will among stockholders or employees when, in fact, it is committed to the business as permanently as that which is termed "capital." For a few corporations, however, the amount of retained earnings is a realistic limitation of the amount available for dividends; the disclosure of the amount of retained earnings in these cases is highly useful information to the stockholder.

Defining the Enterprise for Determining Annual Corporate Net Income

This discussion elaborates somewhat on that in the preceding chapter. There, the separable elements of the enterprise were looked at in terms of risks and potential stability. These considerations are highly pertinent to the stockholder's informational needs about the annual net income of the corporation.

The stockholders being discussed in this book have direct ownership only in that entity which is the parent company. This is a significant fact when consideration is being given to what information is useful to the stockholder about the entire "enterprise." Just as income to the corporation is not income to the stockholder until paid to him in dividends, so in a narrow sense is a subsidiary's income vis-à-vis its parent. This makes the subsidiary's income even more remote from the stockholder of the parent.

It has been developed that the stockholder's principal point of interest is in the corporation's net income. But is this interest only in the parent entity's net income (including only dividends received from subsidiaries)—which is the income nearest to him in availability for dividends—or is it in the income of the entire enterprise? In other words, are the corporate obstacles which subsidiaries' income must surmount to get near the stockholder significant to him or not? Are his informational needs served adequately by financial statements of the parent entity alone, or should he have consolidated statements of the entire enterprise as though corporate lines did not divide the constituent entities? These questions are more easily asked than answered.

Were the stockholder's interest solely in the near-term cash dividends of the corporation, there would be strong reason for his concentrating his interest on the income and liquidity of the parent company alone. Earnings of subsidiaries would not bear directly on his interest until actually realized by the parent. However, as has been seen, the stockholder's interest extends also to undistributed net income as a measure of the increase in the invested capital and, thus, in the corporation's earning power. From this standpoint, just as parent company earnings plowed back into the business are significant to the stockholder, so also are those of the subsidiaries. This approach suggests that the test of realization by the parent of income on its investments in subsidiaries be discarded in favor of a measure of the historical and current earnings rate of the entire enterprise.

In fact, the stockholder must not ignore either consideration: the income of the entire enterprise, or the realization (or prospect of realization) of subsidiary income by the parent. If he should look at parent company realizations alone, he could be misled. Dividends received could for any period of time be more or less than current underlying earnings justify, giving a mistaken view of the real historical trend. The timing and rate of the dividend payments can be influenced by expediencies, or by subjective management decisions, having little relationship to fundamental earning trends.

On the other hand, full consolidation of enterprise earnings has its pitfalls. As was discussed in Chapter II, there are various ways of accounting for parent company investments, depending upon assessments of risk and stability in the underlying situation.

There can be the following shades with respect to the significance of subsidiaries' income to the stockholder of the parent company:

1. At one extreme would be the situation in which a dollar of earnings in the subsidiary is as good as that in the parent. As in the parent, management has discretion as between productive reinvestment or payment of the earnings as cash dividends. No significant tax would attach to the dividend transfer. No cloud is on the horizon threatening these conditions.

2. A middle ground would be that in which the same conditions exist as in (1), except that there are important intervening, but dormant, factors that could affect the power of the parent over the subsidiary or the free flow of dividends to the parent on a dollar-equivalent basis. Examples are: (a) The subsidiary operates in a foreign country whose currency could deteriorate between the time of translating earnings in the foreign currency into dollars for corporate accounting purposes and their actual conversion into the latter currency or the foreign country could restrict or block entirely the conversion of currencies to remit profits; or it could even threaten the continued operation of the subsidiary itself. (b) The subsidiary is under a regulatory or supervisory authority that could intervene in dividend policy. (c) A minority interest exists of the size or type that could inhibit the parent from managing the subsidiary as it otherwise would in the interest of itself and its stockholders. (d) Dividend restrictions in covenants could become effective.

3. At the other end of the scale would be the situation in which the intervening factors, of the type described in (2) as dormant, have or may come alive and importantly alter, if not negate, the thought that the subsidiary's earnings are the dollar-for-dollar equivalent of those of the parent from the standpoint of the latter's stockholders.

In view of the complexities involved in presenting a picture of the enterprise, the stockholder is entitled to and must rely heavily on managment's judgment as to that formula for consolidating subsidiaries (thus treating a dollar of their income like that of the parent) which best accomplishes the desired objective. However, it is evident that in the more complex situations there are imponderables that even the best judgment cannot accurately predict. In these circumstances, the stockholder needs whatever information is available to indicate the shades of uncertainty.

If such doubts as exist have been resolved in favor of consolidating certain subsidiaries to give the best possible picture of the enterprise, the stockholder needs to know how much of the enterprise's picture is made up of the elements surrounded by the uncertainties. (In the United Kingdom, the practice is to go further; a consolidated income statement not accompanied by a separate one for the parent must show how much of the consolidated net income is dealt with in the parent's own accounts.) If doubts have been resolved in favor of not consolidating one or more subsidiaries, or types of subsidiaries, the stockholder needs to know that fact and whatever information exists about the underlying position and results of operations of these entities. This information often can best be supplied by separate financial statements of the unconsolidated subsidiaries. In either case, the stockholder is entitled to some outline of the underlying reasoning of management in making the choice it did.

Occasionally there are instances in which a dollar of a subsidiary's earnings is considered as good for stockholder purposes as a dollar earned by the parent, but consolidation of the subsidiary is still not considered best for stockholder information purposes. Banking and insurance subsidiaries of industrial parents, for example, have patterns of assets, liabilities, income, and expenses so different from those of the parent that commingling of the two types in a consolidation could be more confusing than revealing. In some cases, segregating of homogenous portions of the enterprise within the consolidated statements may be useful. In other cases, not consolidating the subsidiaries, but supplying separate statements if they are significant, may be more informative. In addition, in the consolidation, the investment in the unconsolidated subsidiary may be reported at its current underlying equity, and its current undistributed earnings may be included as a part of the current consolidated earnings. This is the so-called "equity method" of treating investments.

INTERCOMPANY TRANSACTIONS

Stockholder interest in earnings of the enterprise relate to earnings from transactions with parties *outside* the enterprise. Sales among corporate entities within an enterprise are, by this test, incomplete transactions, and any profit therefrom to the selling entity is not yet realized by the enterprise. Transactions among entities within an enterprise are normally canceled out so as to present the stockholder with the results of enterprise transactions with outside parties; if such transactions are for good reasons not canceled out and are significant, the stockholder needs to know about them.

TRANSACTIONS BETWEEN THE CORPORATION AND ITS MANAGEMENT

The stockholder has one other informational need about the corporation—a minor one in the majority of cases in relation to the overall affairs of the corporation. This information has to do with any transactions between the corporation and the individuals who comprise its management. The point has already been made that the identity of the corporation is to be distinguished from that of all other parties, including the corporation's management, which, however, has wide discretionary authority over utilization and disposition of the corporation's resources. Although the individuals comprising management must of necessity divert some of the corporation's resources to themselves as compensation, there is a potential here for a conflict of interest. If feasible, direct approval by stockholders of *unusual* corporate transactions with management, or a formal plan for such, precludes all questions. If these are not feasible, then as in all unusual situations where a question of propriety might arise, full and fair disclosure generally prevents difficulty. The stockholder

is in need of such information, and management is also pro-
tected by the disclosure.

The Stockholder's Responsibilities in Using Corporate Financial Reports

Much has been said of the responsibility resting on the corporation for full and fair disclosure to its stockholders. Although
most of the discussion turns on what the corporation's directors
and management should and should not do with reference to
corporate financial reports, the stockholder's own responsibilities
must also be considered. One responsibility in this respect is to
inform himself of the limitations of the data in portraying the
future, and the other is to appreciate that estimate and judgment,
rather than penny-precision, are behind the data.

The stockholder continually looks to the future. He may focus
on dividend expectations, earnings prospects, or any other aspect
of the corporation's affairs. He may look to the financial statements to help him in his projections. *A stockholder should bear
in mind at all times that financial statements are not designed to
predict the future, but to report on the past and present.* Financial
statements may fairly report constantly increasing earnings for
years, yet the earnings trend may turn down in the next. Or the
reverse may be true.

Naturally, many of the factors that determined past and present results of operations will also affect the future, particularly
in the near-term. These would include management, innovation,
markets, competition, economic trends, and many other internal
and external influences. He who blindly extrapolates results of
the past into results of the future, however, courts trouble. The
question is not whether the *results* of the past are a guide to the
future, but whether the *factors that underlie the results* of the

past will or will not similarly shape the future. One looks outside financial statements for these underlying factors and, having identified them, appraises their effect on the future.

In considering the importance of the words *judgment* and *estimate,* the stockholder should realize that at any one point in time the corporation is host to numerous incomplete transactions. Reporting by periods requires unnatural cuts into the corporate life, and the assignment of net income to specific periods has to rely to some extent on judgment and estimate. To the extent that the assignment reflects sound business judgment and is based upon knowledge of all pertinent facts, it will produce useful data. But effective use of these data requires full knowledge of their limitations and the bases on which they were compiled.

SUMMARY

The stockholder, as the addressee of the corporate financial report, has interests and informational needs that importantly influence the nature and content of the data included therein. Financial analysts and institutional investors will continue to influence disclosure, and will be the most articulate among stockholders and their advisers as to the information required. The fluidity of investors gives rise to the need for corporate reports for short periods of time—unnaturally short in comparison with the long-term commitments and programs of the corporation.

Both the sophisticated and unsophisticated investor are interested in the corporation's historical net income. This can be measured, for a short period, with more reliability for events and transactions that are repetitive than for those that are sporadic and contingent. The stockholder is also interested in the balance sheet, from the standpoint of the light it throws on the income statement, as well as its indication of corporate liquidity. The subdivisions of stockholders' equity in most large corporations are of the least significance and interest of the major portions of the financial statements.

It is a matter of judgment as to what subsidiaries should be consolidated with the parent to give stockholders a single picture of the enterprise. Management has an obligation to make this judgment, but stockholders, in this as in other judgmental areas, have the obligation to digest information submitted about those judgments.

Financial statements are historical in nature; trends therein do not necessarily portend even the near-term future. The stockholder has an obligation not to blindly misuse historical data for extrapolation.

IV

Other External Influences
On Accounting and
Reporting Practices

Most corporations can name specific external parties or factors, in addition to those covered in preceding chapters, that have an effect on their financial accounting and reporting. Some are direct and over-riding, such as accounting requirements (upheld by the courts) of a governmental authority having jurisdiction over a public utility. The impact of formulas for measuring taxable income is another important and widespread influence.

In addition to the social attitude, the nature of the corporation, general environmental conditions, and the views of the stockholder in particular, there are a number of other specific external groups or forces that affect corporate financial account-ing and reporting. They would include such impersonal and per-sonal influences as accounting and reporting precedents set by others, income taxation, creditors, competitors, customers, regu-latory authorities, the courts, and—for international corporations —similar influences in other countries. The impact of each of these factors on corporations varies widely at any given time, and most are continually in a state of change. Accordingly, appropriate adaptation of accounting and reporting practices to these influences becomes largely a matter for study and solution by each corporation or by relatively homogeneous groups of corporations such as those in a clearly defined industry.

Some external influences affect the way the corporation does its business; i.e., they affect the nature, timing, and amount of those transactions or events recorded by accounting. A price reduction by a competitor where the corporation follows suit would be an example, as would a reduction in the income tax rate. In these circumstances, the external effect is already reflected in source documents, the raw material for the accounting (in the examples cited, the sales invoice and the calculation of the accrued income tax for the year). Further accounting problems do not arise from the external event. Other influences, however, have a bearing on the carrying value of a corporation's assets or on the timing of the recognition of revenue and expense items in determining periodic net income. It is these influences that must be taken into consideration in judgments about the appropriateness of a corporation's method of financial accounting and reporting.

INFLUENCE OF THE ACCOUNTING AND REPORTING PRACTICES OF OTHERS

One of the powerful external influences on any given corporation's financial accounting and reporting is the example or precedent set by other corporations in what appear to be similar situations. When faced with making a decision on an accounting or reporting practice, managements often first ask, "What do others do?" Situations sufficiently comparable, so that the research and judgment of others are helpful precedents, can sometimes be identified for corporations as a whole, and even more often for corporations within an industry.

That what others do tends to have a strong influence on the individual corporation can no doubt be attributed to these two important considerations: (1) management's awareness that a number of external parties—including investors, government procurement agencies, income tax authorities, and creditors—make comparisons of accounting practices among corporations; and (2) the preference of management for moving with a consensus rather than risking the criticism attracted by a minority position, particularly if that position is open to attack as self-serving for the short term.

Where two or more accounting practices are in general use in a given subject area, it is pertinent to ask whether the variety of precedents involved tends over a period of time to lower or raise the quality of financial accounting and reporting. It can be postulated, for example, that "competition for current earnings" among corporations forces them to search for support for those accounting practices which result in reporting higher current earnings, with the consequence that later earnings would be lower than otherwise. This approach suggests that opportunistic "bad" practices tend to drive out the "good" ones that are sounder for the long range.

It can be argued, on the other hand, that among corporations there are leaders, many of long standing, whose examples carry more weight than their number suggests. Those stressing this fact point out that the accounting practices of corporate leaders—as in other phases of their operations—are not opportunistic, but rather, have been adapted to the long view with a tendency to be conservative. They believe that the examples set by these corporations have far more influence than those at the other end of the accounting practice scale.

Cases to support either of the foregoing points of view can be drawn from experience. In evaluating the influence of precedents on financial accounting and reporting, therefore, the more pertinent question is whether, on balance, the bad tends to drive out the good, or vice versa. Those accounting precedents that are sounder for the long term tend to prevail, for the simple reason that, with the passage of time, opportunistic practices are frequently exposed as horrible examples. Sudden and unexpected write-offs of huge amounts of capitalized research and development expense, or the collapse of companies that unwisely reported their profits on long-term sales contracts before the collections were reasonably seen to be forthcoming, tend to be dramatic lessons in corporate accounting. Those corporations with the more conservative long-range practices, on the other hand, suffer such shocks rarely—a fact that is not lost on either the investing public or other corporations.

INFLUENCE OF INCOME TAX ACCOUNTING
ON FINANCIAL ACCOUNTING

High income tax rates have an enormous impact on the corporation. Even high rates applicable to individuals and other external parties have an influence on the transactions of the corporation and the decisions of its management, notwithstanding the separateness of the identity of the corporation from all other persons. Thus, the corporation may take an action that will postpone income tax to external parties or make it possible for them to utilize the lower capital gains tax. Examples where this is a factor (not necessarily the controlling one) include: stock distributions in lieu of their market-value equivalent in cash dividends; acquisition of businesses for stock instead of for cash; and compensation of employees in stock options, the right to deferred cash payments, or higher pension rights in lieu of higher current payments in cash. The chief emphasis in this discussion, however, is the influence on the corporation's accounting of the high rate of tax on its *own* taxable income.

The income tax is one of a corporation's costs: just as a corporation cannot manufacture a product without incurring a cost for labor and materials, nor sell it without incurring selling costs, so also it cannot make a profit without incurring an income tax cost. The difference between income tax and most other items of cost is that the latter are measured by the quantity and quality of materials, services, or borrowed money received but the income tax cost is measured by the corporation's profit. The cost is significant: currently, the federal income tax amounts to about one-half of taxable profits.

Because profit is the measure of the tax, some have held that the tax is not a corporation cost but a distribution of corporate profits, i.e., in the same general category as dividends to stockholders. This is a highly questionable position. It suggests that the financially significant index of corporate results is the profit *before* income taxes, and that how this amount is distributed among government, stockholders, and reinvestment is a separable matter. Actually, the stockholder, as a supplier of capital, must look for his return *after* the levy by the government has been paid. If the corporation is to attract new capital, its pricing structure and revenues must be sufficient, after deducting costs including income taxes, to provide the earnings and dividend rates required in the market place.

Income taxation has two important influences on corporate financial accounting. One has to do with the effect of those practices that are acceptable for tax purposes; the other relates to measurement of the annual tax cost itself.

With some exceptions that need not be discussed here, the individual items of revenue and expense which enter into the net income computed for stockholder purposes also enter into the determination of taxable income. Most income and expense items are unquestionably identified with a specific year. These enter into the determination of income in the same year for both tax and stockholder purposes. Concerning those items of income and expense that can be associated with two or more years, the problem of determining both the total number of years to be involved in the apportionment and how much is to be apportioned to each of the constituent years is of course as present in tax accounting as in financial accounting.

The principle originally established for determining periodic taxable income is no different from that for determining stockholder income and, in fact, derives from it. A position taken in the Internal Revenue Code, first inserted in 1916, remains unchanged in substance today. It states: "Taxable income shall be computed under the method of accounting on the basis of which the taxpayer regularly computes his income in keeping his books." A complete survey of accounting practices used for apportioning items of income and expense among years would undoubtedly show that, even where alternatives exist, for the majority of separable issues the method used for stockholder purposes is also used to compute taxable income. The guiding principle taken from business experience and incorporated in the income tax law cited above has been extensively followed.

Not to be overlooked, nevertheless, is the influence in the other direction. Many an accounting practice or measurement method is used today for financial reporting because it has emerged from a controversy between the taxpayer and the income tax authorities, or because it is that method acceptable for tax purposes which produces lower near-term taxable incomes than would alternatives. Not wishing to keep two sets of books, the corporation adopts the tax practice as its own. There is one notable instance in which the influence of income tax authorities has had a far less subtle influence on corporate financial accounting—the use of the "last-in, first-out" (LIFO) inventory method. The LIFO method, as compared with alternative methods, is attractive for computing taxable income in periods of rising prices because it permits the cost of the most recent purchases to be charged against the revenues from sales. However, contrary to custom, income tax law specifies as a condition for using LIFO for tax purposes that this method must also be followed for financial accounting. (Chapter V discusses LIFO as a means of measuring costs to be carried forward to future periods as inventory. It need only be observed here that LIFO is widely used for financial accounting.)

Although there may be more similarities than differences in accounting practices used for tax and financial purposes, it is the differences that create important problems in financial accounting. What is a reasonable measure of the income tax cost applicable to the current year? Many would readily answer: What the income tax return for the year indicates to be payable. However, consider these possible differences between this year's determination of taxable income and the income to be reported to stockholders:

1. The corporation makes a sale on an installment basis with the selling price being collectible over a period of three years. Because the sale is firm and the credit standing of the customer satisfactory, the corporation reports the entire profit as income in the year of sale for stockholder report purposes. The Internal Revenue Service permits the corporation to include in taxable income in the year of sale only that portion of the entire profit which is related to the amount collected during that year; the balance is included in taxable income in future years as collected. Thus, income recognized in the corporate financial report precedes income recognized in the tax return.

2. The corporation has an investment in a nonconsolidated affiliate that has accumulated substantial deficits. The corporation has arrived at the judgment that the impairment is permanent and that, accordingly, it has now identified a loss which it must recognize and report to stockholders. The IRS takes and upholds the position that the loss is deductible for tax purposes only when the loss is realized through disposition of the investment in a manner which gives rise to a tax

deduction. The loss is deducted from income reported to stockholders now, but when the loss will be accepted for tax purposes lies in the indefinite future.

3. The corporation reports to stockholders depreciation on fixed assets over an estimated useful life, and it uses a straight-line method for allocating the cost to each of the years of life, because passage of time is as good an index as any of the rate of exhaustion of the assets. The income tax authorities will allow (and the corporation so elects) for tax purposes that the assets be depreciated over a shorter life than used for financial purposes, and will accept accelerated depreciation methods ("double declining balance" or "sum-of-the-years-digits"). The result is a much higher deduction for depreciation expense in the earlier years of a property's life for taxable than for financial income.

4. Research and development costs are deducted from taxable income as the expenditures are made, but for stockholder reports the corporation defers them to future years when associated revenues are expected.

5. Make-good work on warranties is recognized as a cost for financial purposes in the year of sale on the basis of statistical experience or, when no such experience exists, when the work is known to be required. The costs are allowable as a deduction from taxable income only in the later year during which the work is performed.

6. Pension costs are deductible from taxable income based on payments into funds (within limits) or to pensioners during the year. The amount so paid may be greater, less, or the same as a fair charge against financial income in respect to the year's pension costs.

Setting aside the question of whether there *should* be differences, in the foregoing illustrations the accounting practices for determining periodic taxable and stockholder income *are* different. Because of the differences, in any given year the taxable income will be lower or higher than the pre-tax income reported to stockholders, and the tax payable will be correspondingly lower or higher than if the current tax rate were applied to the financial income. To repeat the earlier question, what is a fair measure of the income tax cost for the year for computing income to be reported to stockholders: the tax actually to be paid for the year, or that which would be payable if stockholder income were also the taxable income?

The dimension of time enters again to frustrate any sweeping answer. If, in relation to stockholder income, every "underpayment" of tax were certain to give rise to an "overpayment" in a future year, the clear answer would be to provide now for the future tax cost. It would be fair to consider that a liability for the future additional tax cost had been created this year and that the cost is therefore attributable to this year. If, to take the other extreme, it is a reasonable premise that the offsetting of this year's tax reduction will never be required, then neither a liability nor a cost has been created; only the tax assessed in this year is then a fair corporate tax cost. This can and does happen when, say, a fleet of automobiles is constantly maintained at the same numerical strength by replacements. The earlier higher deductions for depreciation of a property *unit* under an accelerated method (as compared with straight-line) become lower in its later life but are then offset by higher depreciation on new replacements, with the result that, for the *fleet*, aggregate annual depreciation amounts are the same for the two methods. The initial difference between the two methods is never made up.

There is no question that any enumeration of external influences on a corporation's financial accounting and reporting must place income tax accounting high on the list. Generalizations cannot be made to the effect that this is all bad or all good, for in particular circumstances an income tax method may or may not be appropriate for reporting to stockholders. The influence is there, however.

INFLUENCE OF CREDITORS

Historically, creditors—particularly commercial banks and other lending institutions—have been a strong influence in shaping both the accounting and reporting of corporations. As long as banks have been lending, they have quite naturally desired and

obtained information about borrowers relevant to their relationship, including financial position and operating results. They have
frequently been in a position to specify the nature of the financial
data they desired, the principal accounting practices to be used
in the compilation, and the form in which the data should be
reported.

Perhaps the first significant publication aimed at narrowing
differences in accounting and reporting practices was the pamphlet, *Uniform Accounting*, prepared by accountants, but issued
by the Federal Reserve Board in 1917. This pamphlet, and its
revisions published by the American Institute of Certified Public
Accountants, remained influential for more than two decades. Its
indirect influence continues today. The form for financial statements suggested in the pamphlet is recognizable today, as are
many of the recommended accounting and reporting practices.

The segregation of current assets and current liabilities in
the balance sheet is essentially a banker's notion. At its root is
an indication of the "pounce value" of assets in the event of a
foreclosure of a loan. So is the "cost or market, whichever is
lower" rule for stating inventories or marketable securities, particularly when applied item-by-item, with the result that some
are reduced to market even though, as a whole, market is higher
than cost. If these practices are indications of acceptance of a
banker's point of view in financial accounting and reporting, however, it must be added that the financial statements have by no
means gone all the way in measuring liquidating value. As any
banker knows, receivables, inventories, and many other assets
are properly carried on a "going-concern basis" in a balance sheet
at amounts higher than could be realized in a forced sale.

The foregoing illustration of the banker's influence does not
mean that he is not also interested in the borrower's periodic net
income. He knows from experience that the appearance of large
operating deficits can so change the working capital position that

his chances of loss are greater through foreclosure than by renewal. He thus becomes a "locked-in" creditor, as keenly interested in net income as any stockholder. Along the same lines, the long-term creditor must have a strong interest in net income, for the presence or absence of it is the principal determinant of the future liquid resources available to make repayment. Also, emphasis on the creditor's interest in corporate liquidity does not mean that the stockholder does not have an interest in the same direction; he does.

For financial accounting and reporting of the large, publicly owned corporations, however, it may be said that the creditor influence has gradually tended to be overshadowed by stockholder needs. In essence, this means that a fair determination of periodic income has taken precedence over a fair indication of "pounce value." The assumption of indefinitely long life carries with it the generally valid assumption that no "pouncing" will occur and that, therefore, the accounting need not proceed on the assumption that it will.

It should be added that the creditor usually has a direct and identifiable relationship with the corporation. Certainly this is true of the commercial banker. Even bondholders are personified in a trustee. If these creditors need information different from, or in addition to, that which the corporation supplies to its stockholders in response to their needs, they are in a position to make a direct request and obtain it. In fact, special-purpose financial statements and reports for trustees of bondholders and other creditor interests are frequently prepared.

The conclusion is that the creditor influence on financial accounting and reporting of large, publicly owned corporations to stockholders has an historically significant background, but that it is now clearly subjugated to the prime objective of fairly measuring and reporting periodic income. Where creditor and stockholder informational needs are in conflict, the creditor usually can arrange direct access to the corporation for what he needs to know. At the same time, where his needs and those of the stockholder are the same, the corporate financial report should be so devised as to meet both.

INFLUENCE OF CUSTOMERS

Although customers have, of course, an all-important influence on the economics of a corporation, their influence on corporate accounting as such is rather insignificant. There is one situation, however, in which customers may have a direct impact on the accounting of their supplier: where a contract sales price is on a cost-plus basis and the customer has an important voice in what costs are allowable as a charge against the contract.

Involved here is the question of which costs and expenses incurred during the period should be associated with that period and which should be included in inventories and associated with a future period during which revenues are derived from the contract. Direct association of costs with related revenues is more feasible under cost-plus contracts than under the more common practice of "manufacturing for the shelf." Cost-plus arrangements, for example, may provide that certain of the corporation's costs may not be included in the reimbursement formula under the contract. In such circumstances, even though the costs involved are of a type normally associated with production and carried forward as inventory costs until sale, the argument is strong that they should be treated by the corporation as a cost of the period when incurred. In the opposite direction, cost-plus arrangements may contemplate the recovery in the sales price of research, selling, and general and administrative expenses. Although these items are of a type generally treated as costs of the period when incurred, the arrangements with the customer can provide ample justification for carrying them forward to the period when the corresponding revenues are realized under the contract.

The Department of Defense is currently by far the most important of the customers that influence the accounting of their suppliers in this manner. Its rules and regulations regarding types of costs that it will and will not allow to be associated with military supply contracts and, for some types of allowable costs, the timing of their recognition, are embodied in the Armed Services Procurement Regulations (ASPR) and administrative decisions. Taken together, they constitute quite an accounting system, which differs in many respects from that suitable for the determination of periodic financial income by nonsuppliers to the military.

Some of the provisions of ASPR are questionable, even for the narrow cost accounting purpose for which they are devised. Particularly suspect are those which disregard the integrated nature of a corporation's operations and attempt to carve out portions of the facilities, manpower, materials, and programs of the corporation as the only ones contributing to a contract. An example would be expenses of selling activities to attract civilian business so that productive facilities can be maintained in existence. Evaluations of the measurements of net income by external parties are not under discussion in this book. It is sufficient for the present purpose to say that any corporation, or division thereof, heavily engaged in military production usually has its financial accounting influenced by the contract accounting rules of the Department of Defense.

To the extent that (1) price determinations in military procurement involve both the selection of allowable costs and the use of a rate of allowable profit, and that (2) the supplier's military business is so large that its continuation is important if not essential to successful operation, the Department of Defense becomes quite similar to a rate-making public utility authority in its relationship with the supplier. This would also be true of any other dominant customer following a similar course with respect to a supplier (with the important difference that the customer would then not also be the sovereign). The subsequent discussion of the influence of regulatory authorities, accordingly, is in point here also.

Many of the accounting considerations involved in cost-plus work are also involved in any type of long-term production or construction contract. However, the influence on accounting practices of long-term contracts derives from the nature of the work and transactions involved and, therefore, is not properly included in a discussion of instances in which the *customer* can influence a corporation's accounting.

Influence of Competitors

The point was made earlier that the accounting practices of other corporations may influence the accounting practices of any particular corporation. This influence applies especially to other companies in the same industry, i.e., competitors. In addition to this direct effect, however, the economic consequences to a particular corporation which flow from competitors' actions can also have an indirect influence on its accounting practices. For example, if competitors continually modernize productive facilities, obsolescence becomes a threat, and estimated useful lives for depreciation purposes may well be set shorter than if modernizations were not being carried out by others. Similarly, active and effective research programs by others may strongly suggest that a corporation should not attempt to capitalize research and development expenses and amortize them to future periods, because future sales of the developed product may be reduced or eliminated by competitor action.

It is a fair generalization that the more unstable the competitive environment in which the corporation operates—i.e., the more important the technological changes, the more uncertain the movements in sales prices, the more freely customers switch from one corporation's product or service to another—the heavier the burden of justifying those accounting practices that carry forward past expenditures as balance sheet assets to be amortized against future revenues. If this influence of competitors on the accounting practices of any particular corporation is indirect, it is nonetheless forceful.

Competitors can be a negative influence in one aspect of disclosure. Certain types of financial information are considered by some corporations to be in the nature of proprietary secrets, the dissemination of which might damage their competitive position. Illustrations would include expenditures on research and development, sales or gross profits by product lines or operating divisions, or expenditures by types of advertising. Whether or not the corporation's evaluation of the information as an important competitive secret is reasonable, this restraint on disclosure exists.

INFLUENCE OF REGULATORY AUTHORITIES

Regulatory authorities exert a strong influence on the financial accounting of corporations under their jurisdiction. For some, the control is absolute (subject to the veto power of the courts) and extends all the way to the prescription of a detailed "chart of accounts." For others, the influence is indirect, but not controlling for purposes of the corporate report to stockholders. There are gradations in between.

For purposes of this discussion, regulatory authorities may be divided into two broad groups: (1) those that concern themselves primarily with corporate liquidity, and (2) those that concern themselves with periodic corporate income as such (with the necessary related effect in the balance sheet).

Authorities supervising banks, insurance companies, and other financial institutions have historically tended to require or permit the affected corporations to use those accounting practices which emphasize liquidity. For example, costly fixed assets usable for decades have sometimes been eliminated from the balance sheet or carried at nominal amounts; premiums on bonds may be amortized to maturity but not discounts (amortizing the latter would require *increasing* the carrying value); and costs associated with writing a three-year insurance policy are charged against income immediately, although the premiums are taken into income over the three-year period.

The liquidity approach can distort the annual net incomes of financial institutions, the degree of distortion depending upon the fluctuations among years of the amounts of items such as those described. At the same time, the principal interest of stockholders of the large, publicly owned financial institutions is the same as their interest in any other type of corporation—in net income and dividends. Without minimizing the necessity of the supervisory authorities having information in such form and content as is necessary for the discharge of their responsibilities to the public, it is clear that the supervised corporations should be permitted to adopt those financial accounting and reporting practices that best meet stockholder needs. Currently, there is progress in this direction.

The regulatory authorities that concern themselves with periodic income as such are those that are rate-making—the electric, gas, water, transportation, and communication regulatory bodies. Their approach is to set rates at a level that will produce current revenues sufficient to cover current costs plus a fair return on invested capital. These authorities necessarily concern themselves with the balance sheet to the extent that it reflects those amounts properly carried forward to future periods of operations for regulatory purposes, particularly the items included in "rate base" (principally utility property less accumulated depreciation) for purposes of determining the basis upon which return on invested capital is allowed. The effect of the regulatory authority's attitude (when upheld by the courts) toward assets includable in the rate base can have a dramatic impact upon its financial accounting. An expenditure, say, for fixed assets on which the utility is allowed to earn a continuous return is an asset; one neither includable in the rate base nor otherwise covered in the rate of return is not. Utilities in certain jurisdictions discovered this a number of years ago when they were no longer allowed to include in their rate base the excess of the price paid for going utility concerns over the amortized cost of the acquired properties when first devoted to public service.

The income determination problems of the regulatory authority are of the same fundamental type as those involved in arriving at the corporate income to be reported to stockholders. Again, the central questions are: For those receipts and expenditures (mostly the latter) that must enter into a determination of net income but can be allocated to one or more years, over what total time period should they be assigned and how much to each constituent year? How much should be the annual charge for depreciation, for example, is a perennial question. In recent years, the amount to be included in the current year's "cost of service" (a term frequently used by these authorities) as an income tax cost has been a lively topic. At stake, broadly speaking, is the current level of rates which the utility charges to its customers in comparison with those it will charge at some later period. The more costs allowed now that otherwise would be included later as cost of service, the higher the current rates in comparison with what they would be with greater deferment; the opposite would be true respecting costs and rates in later periods.

The accounting practices of regulatory authorities for distributing income and expenses among periods for rate-making purposes generally are also those which should be used for purposes of reporting to stockholders. The regulatory authority's influence is that direct. The reason is economic. The rate-making process attempts to match revenues and identified costs within relatively brief time spaces and, notwithstanding lags between cost changes and rate actions, is considerably more authoritative as to the amount of costs allocable against the revenues of any given year than would be practices derived from economic experience in unregulated industry. It may often well be that a regulatory authority does not choose the soundest cost distribution methods in its rate-making decisions. However, quarrels on this point must be directed at the rate-making process more than at the suitability of the practices prescribed for determining periodic income to be reported to stockholders.

The foregoing discussion applies to the influence of regulatory authorities on corporate financial accounting practices where the authority is the limiting factor on the revenues of the utility. If the utility cannot earn up to its allowable rate of return because of competition (e.g., certain railroads), then the forces of the market place have replaced the economic power of the regulatory authority over the corporation. If, under these conditions, the rate-making authority continues to prescribe the corporation's accounting methods *as though* it were in control of the rate of return, the financial accounting and reporting for stockholder purposes may well need to depart from the regulatory position and become oriented to the environmental factors that *are* controlling. The recent release of stockholder financial statements from the accounting requirements of the ICC may be a recognition of this fundamental.

For corporations whose rate of return is effectively regulated, the regulatory authority is properly the most important single external influence on their financial accounting. In those cases where rate of return is not effectively regulated, the influence of the regulatory or supervisory authority on corporate financial accounting and reporting has been historically strong, but it should be challenged to the extent that it is suspect as not resulting in a full and fair determination of the periodic income to stockholders.

INFLUENCE OF THE COURTS

Court decisions involving accounting practices are numerous in connection with utility rate-making and the determination of taxable income. Quasi-judicial and judicial determinations also are in the record in connection with accounting regulations and determinations made by military departments and the Renegotiation Board (constituted to recapture overall excessive profits of suppliers under government contracts). Other than in these areas, there are remarkably few court decisions on appropriate and inappropriate accounting practices for corporations, and such as there are usually apply to such extreme or isolated circumstances as paying dividends out of capital.

Thus, it will be observed that there are numerous court cases in which a central authority has attempted to enforce an accounting determination involving an equity as among affected interests. Often, the contentions have been the result of the central authority's attempt to adopt a uniform practice for all situations. However, these centralized determinations are subject to being upset by the courts as not being appropriate in particular cases.

Financial reports to stockholders influence decisions of buyers and sellers of a corporation's stock and could therefore evoke equity questions. The fact that the financial accounting and reporting of large, publicly owned corporations has been the subject of little litigation is revealing. It suggests that an economic purpose is being well served.

INTERNATIONAL INFLUENCES

International influences on corporate financial accounting and reporting stem from two general directions: local environment and international financing.

The international corporation with subsidiaries in many countries will find the accounting and reporting of each subsidiary affected to some extent by local environmental factors of the type described earlier. Since laws, customs, and economic and financial conditions vary among countries, there is naturally a tendency toward development of corresponding differences in accounting and reporting practices. To the extent that the parent can do so without violating local law or otherwise injuring the subsidiary, it usually imposes on the latter its own accounting and reporting practices. The international influence is direct. Differences that cannot be eliminated in this manner are sometimes adjusted by the parent company for purposes either of preparing consolidated statements or compiling separate summaries for stockholders of the position and results of operations of foreign interests.

The flow of capital across national boundaries, other than via the international corporation, constitutes a further international accounting influence. Commercial and investment bankers sending capital abroad need financial statements that are comprehensible to them in form and content. They tend to look askance at any practices current in the borrower's country which result in a significantly different financial position or amounts of historical net income than would result from the practices followed in their own country.

The effect of international flows of capital on financial accounting and reporting is easily discerned when a foreign corporation makes a public sale of securities in the United States. These must be registered with the SEC, which requires that the prospectus report the effect on net income of deviations from accounting practices generally accepted in the United States. Again, the creditor nation's practices cross international boundaries.

There is a growing interest in the differences in corporate financial accounting and reporting among the industrial nations. These differences may be seen as historical accidents or the result of differing environmental factors. Some who studied the problem are already suggesting the potential usefulness of world-wide accounting standards. Pressures in this direction will increase in proportion to increases in the international cross-flow of capital, particularly through public sales of securities.

SUMMARY

The financial accounting and reporting of any corporation is subject to a variety of external influences. Some may affect a number of similarly situated corporations in much the same way; others have impacts that must be measured corporation by corporation. Taken together with more general environmental influences and the specific interests of the stockholder, these external influences present such a variety of facts and circumstances as to preclude the formulation of more than a few universally applicable conclusions. A larger number of common approaches to accounting and reporting problems can be found in a given industry or other relatively homogeneous group of corporations than in all of industry. A significant proportion of the responsibility for fair financial accounting and reporting must continue to rest with each corporation's management; the interrelationship of its operations and programs with external influences will continue to make each corporation different from every other.

V

The Measurement Process: Accounting for Repetitive Operations

Considering the magnitude and long-range nature of many of the corporation's commitments, and also the stockholder's interest in reports of its periodic income, the central problem of corporate accounting is the measurement of revenues and expenses for short periods of time. To meet this problem in connection with repetitive transactions and events, there have been developed out of long experience four general guides to assist in making decisions: the *transaction guideline*, the *matching guideline*, the *systematic and rational guideline*, and the *nondistortion guideline*. The application of these to major classes of revenue and expense shows that often judgment is involved in giving one more weight than another. Consistency in measurement method and technique is of great importance.

The preceding chapters have uncovered a number of needs and influences to which financial accounting and reporting should be responsive. This chapter deals with responsiveness to those needs and influences in terms of accounting guidelines and practices in the measurement process.

The distinct interest of the stockholder in the corporation's periodic net income has been discussed. Essentially, this makes the central measurement problem within the accounting function the assignment of a corporation's revenues, costs, gains, and losses to a given year. Some idea of the magnitude of the problem may be obtained by looking at the statement of financial position of the hundred large industrial corporations in the Appendix. The various items may be regrouped according to whether the next step regarding them is normally direct conversion to cash, or amortization as charges or credits in the income statement, as seen in the table on the opposite page.

Note that two-thirds of the items on the asset side of the balance sheet—some $42 billion out of a total of $63 billion—are not assets in the sense of either being or expected to be directly converted to cash. They represent a huge amount of "deferred costs," mostly past cash expenditures, which are to be included as costs in future income statements. They are equivalent to nine years' net income at the current rate of the hundred large industrial corporations referred to in the Appendix. Among all the footnotes explaining and elaborating on the income statement, this makes the balance sheet the biggest footnote of all. In contrast to the importance of deferred costs, it will be observed from the above summary that deferred credits in the balance sheet are not large, either in relation to other amounts in the balance sheet or amounts in the income statement. This contrast highlights the fact that the apportioning of costs among several years is a much greater problem than that of apportioning credits.

The above-described items of deferred costs and deferred credits in the balance sheet arise from the use of the accrual basis of accounting. As stated in Chapter II, this approach is to be contrasted with the cash basis of reporting. To repeat, the accrual basis attempts to transfer the income and expense effect of cash receipts and disbursements, other transactions, and other events from the year in which they arise to the year or years to

ASSETS

	Millions	%
Cash and to be converted to cash:		
Cash	$ 2,495	
Securities	5,458	
Receivables		
Short-term	8,419	
Long-term	490	
Other assets	886	
	$17,748	28%
To be deducted from future income:		
Inventories[a]	$ 9,554	
Prepaid expenses	225	
Deferred charges	230	
Fixed assets[b]	31,867	
	$41,876	67
To remain in present state:		
Business investments[c]	$ 3,050	
Goodwill and intangibles[d]	223	
	$ 3,273	5
	$62,897	100%

LIABILITIES

	Millions	%
To be paid from cash:		
Current liabilities	$10,136	
Long-term debt	7,129	
Provisions (reserves)	970	
	$18,235	29%
To be added to future income:		
Deferred income taxes[e]	$ 318	
Deferred credits	355	
	$ 673	1
To remain in present state:		
Minority interest	$ 685	
Stockholder's equity	43,304	
	$43,989	70
	$62,897	100%

[a] For some portion the classification is near "to be converted to cash," but a step of deriving revenue from a sale intervenes.

[b] Includes land which will not be deducted from future income. Amount not available, believed minimal.

[c] Some portion could be converted to cash or deducted from future income.

[d] Some is being deducted from income, but the portion is not readily ascertainable.

[e] A portion not determinable but perhaps large may be assignable to the section "to remain in present state."

which they more rationally relate. The cash basis treats them as income or expenses when they arise.[1]

The accrual basis reflects the fact that the corporation's activities progress much more evenly over the years than its cash outflow and inflow. It avoids the haphazard distortions of net income by years which would result if the cash basis were used and, say, the entire cost of each manufacturing plant were considered an expense of the year it was acquired, even though it would be used for many years, or build-ups of inventory were treated as an expense this year rather than the next, in which they are sold. The accrual basis is not applied in practice as extensively as pure theory would suggest, however. As will be seen, the theory continually runs afoul of limitations on the ability to predict the future—to foresee, for example, whether this year's expenditures that *should* benefit the future actually *will* and, if so, by how much. In spite of these limitations, however, the accrual basis of accounting stands always as an indispensable enabling authority for avoiding the reporting of distortions in year-to-year corporate income, when the facts are that a corporation's activities and operating results progress more evenly than its cash transactions would indicate.

General Guidelines for Allocating Revenues and Expenses to Periods

The theory of the accrual basis of accounting is too general to provide a basis for making decisions in many situations.

---

1. A pure cash basis of accounting is not even allowed for federal income tax purposes. The income tax regulations provide that even under the cash receipts and disbursements method for the computation of taxable income, constructive receipt of income will be recognized. While expenditures are generally to be deducted for the taxable year in which actually made, if an expenditure results in the creation of an asset having a useful life that extends substantially beyond the close of the taxable year, such expenditure may not be currently deductible in full.

Further guidelines are needed in practice. Also, the uncertainties of the future sometimes render the usefulness of applying the theory nebulous, if not doubtful, thus further emphasizing the need for guidelines.

The Transaction Guideline

Record the effect on net income of transactions and events in the period in which they arise unless there is justification for recording them in some other period or periods.

In the application of the accrual basis of accounting, actual experience indicates that a majority of the items of income and expense are recorded as such in the year of the relevant cash receipts and disbursements. For example, a comparison of the revenues of $67.3 billion of the hundred large industrial corporations in the Appendix with $8.4 billion in accounts receivable at the year's end, suggests that some seven-eighths of the reported revenues were represented by sales both effected and collected during the year. Of the total costs and expenses of $62.6 billion, the indication is that approximately 80 per cent were established by cash expenditures or current liabilities during the year.

It is instructive to pursue further the analysis of the data for the hundred corporations to estimate the revenues, expenses, and net profit that would have resulted if a strict cash basis had been used. This would have required all expenditures for inventories, fixed assets, and the like to be expensed immediately and revenues to be measured by cash collections on sales. On the cash basis, revenues and total costs and expenses would not have varied by more than 1 to 2 percent. However, the leverage would have produced a much sharper change on the residual net income figure. Individual companies would, of course, show divergencies of different magnitudes.

The foregoing indicates that a high percentage of business

transactions are reported as revenues or expenses in the income statement at the time of the *cash transactions,* or near that point in time. True, many sales or purchases are on credit, but most of these are near to the cash receipt or disbursement—near in the sense that the collection of the receivable or the liquidation of the obligation occurs well within the conventional accounting period of one year. The income statement, then, starts out by largely reflecting *transactions,* and this means, predominantly, *cash transactions.* At the same time, the analysis of the data from the hundred corporations indicates that there can be a sharp difference in *net income* for as short a period as one year through departing from the transactions in applying the accrual basis of accounting.

What this amounts to is that financial accounting, in recording the progress of the corporation, looks for objective evidence of that progress. The most emphatic evidence which it can obtain that the corporation has earned revenues, for example, is to observe that it has received cash from an outside party in payment of products delivered or services rendered. But if the corporation has received only a *promise to pay,* rather than cash, financial accounting must set about to assess the probability that the cash will ultimately be received. Accrual accounting will permit the corporation to report that it has earned revenues upon the delivery and acceptance of the product or services if the credit term is short and the credit experience with the customer is good.

However, if experience and prospects suggest that only 99.5 per cent of the customers' promises to pay will be received in cash, then this phase of accrual accounting gives way to the cash basis and admonishes that the 0.5 per cent should not be recognized as corporation revenues unless and until all collections are made. The longer the deferral of the cash receipt from the point of sale, the more the dimension of time introduces uncertainties. For example, assume that a significant portion of a corporation's operations consists of 20-year installment sales of real estate, that risks are not widely spread, and that the corporation has no long-term collection experience. Under these circumstances, even though the corporation had completed its operating cycle when the agreements were signed with the customer, the accrual of profit at the time of sale would probably give way to the reporting of income on the practical cash basis of realization—the actual collection of the installments.

The tug of war between the accrual basis of accounting and the cash transaction works the same way, in reverse, on corporation costs. Whether an expenditure be for inventories, investments, deferred charges, research and development, fixed assets, or the like, the cash disbursement ordinarily precedes the expected benefit. The objective evidence is that disbursements of cash have been made for materials, labor, or services which sooner or later are unquestionably to be charges against the income of the corporation. The question is, income-charge now or later? Since the corporation has already given up some of its resources by the disbursement of its cash (which is objective evidence that it may have incurred a current cost), the pressure becomes strong to demonstrate why and how the expenditure will be a benefit to future years rather than a charge against the present.

The accrual basis of accounting, as well as other specific guidelines discussed below, provides ample justification in practice for reporting cost incidence not in the year of the cash disbursement but in the years of benefit. The alternative guidelines also provide for anticipating future cash disbursements in respect of current costs, such as services being received now which are to be paid for later.

The foregoing discussion has centered on transactions. Financial events that are not transactions also must receive accounting recognition at some point in time, either at the point of the event or at some other appropriate time. A catastrophe causing damage or the signing of an agreement settling a claim are events which, like the transaction, call for an appropriate accounting when they happen, unless the burden is borne of justifying an accounting for them in other periods.

THE MATCHING GUIDELINE

> *Where a direct relationship between the two exists, match costs with revenues.*

One guideline which is highly persuasive in departing from the transaction guideline is that of matching revenues with related costs and reporting them in the same year. The application of the guideline is clearly seen in a merchandising operation, where merchandise is purchased this year but not sold until the next. The carrying forward of the inventory of unsold merchandise so as to offset its cost against the revenue from its sale is clearly useful in determining the net income of each of the two years. Numerous other related events can be, and are, matched in business experience. For example, the effecting of a sale can be matched with a liability to pay a sales commission.

Although there are cases in which the matching guideline is clearly useful, its application is much more restricted than one might think. It must be remembered that matching attempts to make a direct association of costs with *revenues*. The ordinary business operation is so complex that revenues are the end product of a variety of corporate activities, often over long periods of time; objective evidence is lacking to connect the cost of most of the activities with any particular revenues.

The matching guideline is sometimes confused with the allocation of costs to periods. Taxes, insurance, or rent, for example, may be paid in advance and properly allocated to the years covered. However, this allocation is to a *period*, and one would be hard pressed to establish any direct connection between—i.e., to match—these costs and specific sales of the period to which they are allocated.

Even with respect to inventories (the best illustration of the usefulness of the matching guideline) some costing methods tend to dilute the purity of the approach. Thus, while from the standpoint of the physical movement of most products or merchandise it is usual for the oldest items to be sold first, the "last-in, first-out" inventory costing method will offset against a sale the cost of the *last* item added to inventory. If LIFO has been in effect for 20 years, the costs of the items in this year's inventory may be those of items acquired 20 years ago—and, physically, long since gone.

The matching guideline, so highly persuasive as virtually to be controlling when an objective basis for it exists, is, as a basis of apportioning revenues and costs among periods of time, limited in practice to relatively few types of items. The matching guideline can become potentially dangerous when it attempts to match *today's real costs* with *hopes of tomorrow's revenues,* as in deferring research and development costs to be matched against hoped-for, but speculative, future revenues.

THE SYSTEMATIC AND RATIONAL GUIDELINE

> *Where there is justification for allocating amounts affecting net income to two or more years, but there is no direct basis for measuring how much should be associated with each year, use an allocation method that is systematic and rational.*

More revenues and expenses can be associated with *time periods* than with each other. Some items are clearly applicable to specific total periods of time. Prepaid taxes, insurance, and rent have already been mentioned. Advance subscriptions to periodicals could be added, as could payments for patents, bonus payments to acquire leaseholds, and leasehold improvements (all have definite expiration dates). For all these, and many other items, it is clearly rational to translate the relative cash receipts or disbursements into revenues or expenses applicable to two or more years, rather than solely to the year of the transaction.

There are other expenditures that equally clearly will be used or useful in future productive operations, but the total time period involved cannot be accurately predicted. The various categories of fixed assets are illustrations: buildings, machinery, equipment, and other such facilities. Outside limits can be indicated by estimated physical life—the point at which they will collapse beyond repair. *Useful* life will ordinarily fall short of this, the earlier replacement being indicated by (1) the increasing cost of repairs and maintenance in the later stages of life; (2) greater efficiencies of newer facilities; (3) other technological obsolescence; or (4) improved facilities placed in service by competitors. The estimated useful life (with recognition of obsolescence) of long-term facilities is of necessity a matter of broad estimate—an estimate required to be made at the beginning of a long period of time but, by its nature, requiring periodic reassessment.

Thus far the discussion has dealt with the total period of time over which certain corporation expenditures should be allocated. There remains the question of how much should be allocated to each of the short yearly periods of time. If the total period of time with which past expenditures should be associated is a matter of broad estimate, surely that portion of the expenditures allocable to each of the intervening years is more so.

Financial accounting sets up an important guideline for attacking problems of this type: the method chosen must be systematic and rational. There are many applications for this guideline, but the important one of depreciation will serve as an illustration.

Having established the total period over which the costs of fixed assets are to be amortized, and with the fixed-asset cost known, the question is: What systematic method for allocating a portion of the total cost to each year is the most rational in relation to the corporation's operations, policies, and programs? The principal methods actually used by companies are these:

1. The "straight-line" method, which charges an equal amount of depreciation against revenues each year. The rationale is that the passage of time is as good a measure as any of the expiration of the cost.

2. Accelerated methods ("double declining balance" and "sum-of-the-years digits"), which result in higher depreciation charges in earlier years and lower depreciation charges in later years of the property life. The classic rationale is that maintenance and repair costs are higher in the later years, offsetting the lower depreciation costs and giving a more even annual total property cost over a property's life. Another argument for this method is that newer equipment has greater utility than older equipment. A contributing factor sometimes is a potential threat of obsolescence even earlier than that considered in originally setting the useful life.

3. A "use" method, which charges depreciation at a fixed amount per unit of output or similar measure of use. Annual depreciation charges then fluctuate in proportion to the volume of activity. The rationale is that the fixed assets exist to further the economic activity involved and that their cost, therefore, should be apportioned to years based upon use. (The method involves estimating total units of use—for example, number of pieces to be produced by a machine tool—during its useful life, which is difficult to do with assurance. This requirement for an additional estimate may account for the fact that the method is used less than the other two.)

The straight-line method—apportionment based upon the expiration of time alone—is widely used for items other than fixed assets, such as prepaid or deferred taxes, interest, insurance, rents, and other costs where payments pertain to more than one year.

The systematic and rational guideline is applicable, then, in situations where there is no other more practical approach for determining how much of a total should be apportioned to each of several years. In these situations, the conditions are such that even judgments about appropriate annual amounts would have so little foundation as to be considered arbitrary. The guideline rules out subjective and varying judgments as to the portion of the total cost to be absorbed from year to year, and it avoids the attendant suspicions that would be aroused as to the objectivity with which applicable amounts in corporate income statements have been determined.

THE NONDISTORTION GUIDELINE

> *From among systematic and rational methods, use that which tends to minimize distortions of periodic net income.*

It has been mentioned earlier that the corporation's programs, commitments, and activities are typically directed at long periods of time and that they tend to progress much more evenly than cash receipts and expenditures. It has also been observed that periodic income determined under the accrual basis of accounting more faithfully reflects this relative steadiness in a corporation's progress, as compared with what would be obtained if annual income were the net result of each year's cash receipts and disbursements alone.

There are specific allocation practices that are designed to avoid or minimize distortions of net income among years. Illustrations include:

1. With self-insurance provisions, a corporation may become a self-insurer for, say, its fleet of vessels, or its plants, facilities, or stores at a number of locations. Such a corporation may charge annual income with level amounts, perhaps equal to the premiums that would otherwise be paid to outside insurers, and accumulate these amounts in a reserve until it is at least as great as that required for a major disaster. Beyond that point it may hold the reserve at a rather level amount in relation to the covered assets, so that the income is there-

after charged for the nondistorting recurring losses. If a major disaster does occur and is charged against the reserve, the reserve is then gradually built up again.

2. Something of the same approach can be seen in many practices of providing for bad debts. The identity of those out of the current group of customers who will not pay their debts cannot be ascertained (otherwise, credit would not be extended to them), yet past experience indicates that a certain percentage of sales will not be collected. Where bad debt experience is repetitive and made up of small amounts, provisions for the purpose are made by deducting amounts from current revenues based upon a kind of moving average of recent past experience, modified by rational expectations of changes in near-term future experience. However, where bad debt losses are sporadic and involve sizable amounts, statistical experience has less validity and the "major disaster" approach is the better way of avoiding distortions in periodic net income.

3. Provisions may be made for amortization of periodic significant costs. Certain costs of sizable amounts are incurred rather regularly, but at intervals of several years. Examples from past experience include the dry-docking of ships for major overhauls or the relining of blast furnaces. Unless the number of property units involving these costs is so large that actual annual expenditures for the costs are relatively steady, accounting for the costs in the year in which the work is performed would tend to distort income. A rational practice is to spread the costs over a reasonable period of time.

Still other allocation practices that have the effect of minimizing distortions of net income are those which measure the charge to each year's income by the volume of some related activity. One such practice is the "use" method, already described as a depreciation method recognized as meeting the test of being systematic and rational. Another closely related practice concerns the costs associated with underground mineral resources, such as lease and well costs of petroleum companies. These are typically amortized by annual charges to income in proportion to the fraction of the estimated total of the accessible and economically recoverable underground resources which is extracted each year.

The reason use or activity methods of apportioning costs

among periods act to minimize distortion of net income among periods is perhaps obvious, but it deserves emphasis. It is a fair generalization that the increase or decrease in most corporations' revenues and in the use of their facilities are directly related. If the facilities' costs are equal among years, while revenues fluctuate, then net income fluctuates more violently than the revenues because of the "fixed" (i.e., equal as among years) calculation of the facility cost. If the costs of facilities fluctuate roughly in sympathy with revenues, income distortions are lessened.

A partial reconciliation is possible among the transaction, the systematic and rational, and the nondistortion guidelines. Corporations include in the computation of net income for the year some amounts that benefit future periods. Advertising and other promotional expenditures are examples. How can the three guidelines be reconciled here? The answer is that, for repetitive operations of a going concern operating at a fairly consistent level, the transaction guideline also is systematic and rational, and produces a nondistorted effect. It is only when the level of transactions changes sharply upward or downward that the effects of the guidelines would differ; then judgment must be applied in selecting an appropriate guideline.

It should be emphasized here that this discussion of nondistortion accounting methods should be kept in context. What has been under consideration is accounting for repetitive transactions and events and the allocation of revenues and costs associated with these. The discussion should not be considered as suggesting that the effect of unusual gains or losses be hidden (these are discussed later); nor should it be thought to suggest that fluctuations of revenues and costs directly related to particular periods should be disguised in any way.

Four guidelines have been cited as useful in the application of the accrual basis of accounting in measuring the financial position and results of operations of a corporation, namely, transaction, matching, systematic and rational, and nondistortion. Obviously, because these guidelines can be in conflict in particular situations, judgment is often involved as to the emphasis to be given to each. Some illustrations of applications of the guidelines to specific problems have been given, but others may be added in connection with items appearing in the conventional form of corporate financial statements.

Application of the Guidelines

Throughout the subsequent discussion, it will be noted that the amounts at which many assets and liabilities are stated in the balance sheet are a by-product of methods designed to produce a fair periodic net income figure. The objective is *not* to produce a liquidating value or a current fair market value of assets. This approach is consistent with the primary interest of the stockholder in periodic income, as opposed to liquidating or "pounce" values in a not-to-be-liquidated enterprise.

MEASURING REVENUES, OTHER GROSS INCOME, AND GAINS

The guideline of orientation to the transaction or event dominates the accounting for most revenues. There are two significant events related to the recording of revenues by an industrial company: the effecting of the sale (delivery by the corporation and acceptance by the customer) of a completed product or service, and the collection of the resulting receivable.

The sale is predominately used as the point in the operating cycle at which revenue is recorded. Corporate experience is generally such that, with only minor allowances for uncollectable accounts, collection may be expected to follow in due course and therefore is not as significant an event as that of effecting the sale. There are important exceptions, however, in which the collection becomes the more dominant of the two events. The example has been alluded to of a corporation engaged in selling on the long-term installment basis—as in real estate—where there may not have been sufficient experience for assuming future collections. In such cases, the gross profit from the sales, if not the revenue itself, is not recognized until installments are collected. If sales on a long-term collection basis tend to fluctuate materially from year to year, the nondistortion guideline may also support the collection as the point for recognizing revenues.

Note that the matching guideline does not usually effect the timing for recognizing revenues. In practice, the decision as to when to record revenues is made first; any costs which can be matched with these are then shifted accordingly. An exception to this practice, however, often is observed for long-term production under contract—for example, the building of a ship or a dam. Here, the contract of sale has been executed before production commences, and the credit of the customer is considered such that ultimate collection presents no problem. The nondistortion guideline may dictate that, in these circumstances, the so-called percentage-of-completion method be used, under which revenue is recognized as the relative costs are accumulated. Thus, revenue is matched with costs rather than costs with revenue. (The propriety of this method is subject to the reliability with which total ultimate costs, and therefore the degree of progress at any interim point, can be estimated.)

Whether long-term production or long-term collection is involved, however, the force of the nondistortion guideline is importantly affected by the frequency and relative size of the transactions involved. Thus, a corporation with large numbers of constantly recurring production contracts extending over more than one year may, without distorting the corporation's periodic income, be able to defer the recognition of revenue until the completion of each contract. The same applies to recognizing revenues at the point of sale where large numbers of installment contracts continually recur, giving both evenness to a trend and a reasonable basis for predicting collections.

In these cases, viewing transactions in the aggregate can lead to a different conclusion than if each were considered separately. This appraisal of the net result from an aggregation of like transactions or events, rather than each individually, occurs over and over again in corporate financial accounting. It is frequently a means of conforming to the nondistortion guideline and is in harmony with the facts of the business operation itself.

Notwithstanding the exceptions discussed above, it must be remembered that most revenues are recognized at the point of sale which, in turn, is near the point of the cash collection. As compared with any alternative under which revenue would be accrued as production proceeds and goods are put on the shelf for sale, the practice is conservative.

Despite this conclusion, one should not consider that conservatism dictated the practice, that the result was the cause. From the viewpoint of the stockholder—or, for that matter, society in general—the corporation's operating cycle is not concluded until a sale is effected. The corporation's resources that were expended in the production process are not replenished until that point is reached and the cash is collected. These are the last steps in the operating cycle. That revenues are not recognized and reported to stockholders until the last conceivable point in time happens to meet the test of conservatism, but the fundamental issue is that it harmonizes with the realities of corporate operation and informational needs of stockholders.

This practice of delaying recognition of earned revenues can be described another way: unrealized increments in value usually are not reported as corporate income. For example, long-term business investments may clearly have appreciated in value; or land, used in operations but not consumed in the process, may now be worth far more than its original cost; or minerals worth many times the amount expended for discovery may have been proven. In situations such as these, it is logical to ask: Should not corporate net income include appreciation as it takes place, whether or not it is realized? The question has already been discussed in connection with stockholder informational needs, where it was concluded that the inclusion in net income of unearned increments would not enhance the usefulness of financial statements to him. In this discussion of the measurement process, however, some observations may be added.

With respect to the recognition of unrealized gains, the transaction guideline and that of nondistortion are again in conflict. The transaction guideline is persuasive where disposition of the asset and realization of the appreciation either is not contemplated at all or is, at best, a contingency more or less remote in time. Where disposition is a more reasonable expectancy, but fluctuations in the market value are such that the *amount* of appreciation, if any, ultimately to be realized is uncertain, the emphasis changes to that of uncertainty of amount. Under either of these circumstances, corporate financial accounting will usually conclude that enhanced value should be reflected only as realized, either in higher periodic earnings from the asset or upon its actual disposition. (Disclosure of useful information about unrealized appreciation is another matter; this is discussed in Chapter VII.)

Where appreciated assets are frequently liquidated, however, the guideline of avoiding distortions of net income sometimes comes into play. Investment trusts, for example, price their portfolios at market—appreciated or not. The nondistortion guideline also justifies periodic increases in the amount of investments in unconsolidated subsidiaries to the amount of underlying net assets and thus permits combining their periodic net income with that of the parent company. Despite these exceptions, however, the general practice is that recognition of appreciation in assets as corporate income awaits a transaction or event signaling its realization.

MEASURING COST OF GOODS SOLD

The matching guideline calls for deducting costs directly associated with products or services sold from the revenues derived from the sale. The nondistortion guideline reinforces the precept. Thus, the automobile dealer who buys a car in one year and sells it in the next should match the car's purchase cost with the revenue from its sale in the latter year. Tugging in the other direction, however, is the transaction guideline, which dictates that the cost should be associated with the period in which it arises, unless the association of revenue and cost is direct. Accordingly, a portion of the rent, taxes, insurance, and maintenance of the showroom, which theoretically might be allocated to the cost of exhibiting the car, is less tangibly related to the sale and, therefore, is treated as a cost of the period in which incurred.

If a doubt can arise as to the matching of costs with revenues in the simple circumstances of the automobile dealer, it can be multiplied a thousandfold for the corporation with more complex operations. The basic questions are two: First, which costs should be associated with the items *added* to the inventory? Second, of the costs added to the inventory, which should be associated with items withdrawn from the inventory and sold during the year? It may surprise most laymen that the second of these two questions exists, for they may visualize a kind of "cost tag" attached to each inventory item which would readily yield the cost to be removed from inventory when the item is sold. This is not the way most inventories work. Rather, a mass of costs is accumulated in the accounting records for a mass of physical items comprising an inventory group. As will be seen, this fact leaves room for more than one systematic and rational method of associating costs with products sold.

Measuring costs added to inventory. As to the first question, the association of costs with items added to an inventory during the year is not as simple as might be believed. Reaching this state in a corporation's operating cycle is actually the result of administration, financing, research, development, acquisition of facilities, development of markets, and other activities of the corporation. The costs of all these activities will have contributed to some extent to the ultimate realization of revenues and therefore, in theory, could be considered part of the "cost of goods sold," which is offset against revenues. However, practical considerations intervene. Uncertainties arise as to whether present efforts *will* contribute to future revenues and, even if that is established on an objective basis, whether the ultimate revenues will be sufficient to cover all such costs.

A fair, generalized explanation of the inventory costing methods used by corporations is that the activity which gives rise to an inventory cost must be *physically* associated with the item added to inventory; otherwise, the transaction guideline dictates that the costs are associated with the period in which they occur. Thus, the costs of materials directly entering into the finished product, and of labor expended in fabricating and assembling it—which touches it, so to speak—should clearly be included in inventory. At the other end of the scale, the costs of those activities remote from the plant in which the product is produced, such as advertising, should not.

There remains a gray area of costs, often significant in amount, where the matching and transaction guidelines are in conflict. Most of the overhead costs in a factory are in this category: plant administration, personnel, purchasing, accounting, warehousing, scheduling, supervision, and the depreciation and maintenance of facilities. Many of these costs are fixed in that their amounts change little regardless of quantities produced. Others are semi-variable, in that they fluctuate only with wide and somewhat prolonged swings in production volume and generally react somewhat tardily to new volume levels.

A systematic and rational method for choosing those semi-variable costs that are to be added to inventory and carried forward to be matched with revenues from the subsequent sale, and those that are to follow the transaction guideline to become costs of the period, is best devised for each different production and merchandising operation. Which activities can sustain the burden of argument that they add value to the product or service produced, and which fail in this respect and should become costs of the period, must rest upon an appraisal of actual operations. Not a small part of the judgment in actual circumstances will also derive from the guideline to choose a method that tends to minimize distortions in periodic net profit and this, in turn, will probably turn on the volume and frequency of repetitive transactions and events.

The discussion of input of costs into inventory may be concluded with the observation that the applicable guidelines tend to exclude far more "gray area" costs from inventory than are included. The result is that the amounts added to inventory do not purport to be a fair market or other such economic value of the inventory items and, in fact, are usually below any such amounts. A commendable consequence of this, however, is that income distortions are minimized through fewer broad-scale inventory write-downs when sales prices fall or markets shrink.

Measuring costs taken out of inventory. The second basic question in connection with matching cost of goods sold with the related revenues, given the costs added to inventory, is: Which of the costs included in the inventory are to be associated with the items removed from it as sales are made? For a minor portion of corporate activity, costs *are* identified with specific inventory items, with the result that revenues and costs of the specific item sold are matched directly. This usually applies to large, custom-built inventory items, such as special-purpose equipment and construction projects built under contracts.

By far the larger portion of corporate inventories consists of mass-produced items classified into groups. For these, as has been said, each item does not carry a cost tag; in fact, little useful purpose would be served by the costly clerical process that would be required if it did. Rather, there are recorded the unit costs of items added to the inventory for a given period, such as a day, month, or year. With these statistical records, *assumptions* are made as to the costs to be associated with the units delivered out of the inventory for sale. The most prevalent of these assumptions in corporate practice are:

1. The costs of the oldest items in inventory are to be associated with the items delivered. This is the so-called "first-in, first-out" (FIFO) method. Its rationale is that it is usual business practice to deliver the oldest items first to avoid obsolescence or deterioration.

2. The average of the costs of items at the beginning of a period and those added during the period are to be associated with the items delivered ("average cost"). The rationale here is that there is a commingling of old and new items in the inventory, and chance determines which one is delivered. Where acquisition costs tend to fluctuate, the average-cost method minimizes swings in unit costs within the inventory. If sales prices do not move in sympathy with the acquisition costs, this method also minimizes fluctuations in gross profit.

3. The costs of the latest items added to inventory are to be associated with the items delivered. This "last-in, first-out" (LIFO) method departs from normal assumptions as to physical operating conditions and derives mostly from the effects of changing prices. The rationale is that, in periods when rising price levels push up selling prices, the "pushed up" costs should be matched against the revenues, and these would ordinarily be the most recent costs; similarly with falling prices. This theory suggests that, under other methods during periods of rising prices, for example, inflated revenues are matched against less inflated

costs. The result is that constantly increasing amounts are included in inventories for the same quantities, whereas the inflated amounts have already been recovered from inflated selling prices. (In periods of rising prices, the LIFO inventory method results in an even more radical understatement of balance sheet inventory amounts, in relation to the "current market" or "economic" values thereof, than the other-named inventory methods.)

Of the above-described three inventory methods, LIFO is the most recent to come into widespread use beyond the extractive industries.[2] Since extension of its use coincided with liberalization of its allowability for federal income tax purposes, it seems clear that one of its great attractions to corporations is that, under inflationary conditions, it reduces taxable income (and the outflow of corporate cash for taxes) as compared with the other inventory methods. The federal taxation law requires that LIFO be used for reporting to stockholders if it is used for tax purposes. If it were not for this requirement, it is doubtful if the method would be used so extensively in financial accounting, for these reasons: the unrealistically low inventory amounts sometimes produced in the balance sheet; nonconformity with the business practice of selling the oldest items first, where there is a choice; and the occasionally distorted increases of net income which result from dipping into the older, low-cost inventory blocks when sales sharply outrun production.

As the foregoing discussion suggests, beyond a few industries where it is well suited for other reasons, LIFO's principal justification for use in financial accounting is that it removes part of the inflation of corporate net income due solely to a rising price level. As such, it follows less the guidelines for other measure-

---

2. However, its effects closely resemble the "base stock" method, now in rare use but used years ago by some companies, particularly where primary metals subject to wide price gyrations were involved. The "base stock" method assumed that specified minimum quantities were required to be maintained in inventory merely to remain in business, and that these should be kept at uninflated historical prices (some low point reached in past fluctuations).

ments of corporate net income (except for being systematic and rational) than one that might be stated thus: Eliminate from corporate net income that amount estimated to be the result of changes in the general price level, as opposed to being the net result of the corporation's own operations. This latter might well be a useful guideline for measuring corporate net income, but it has not yet found general support among parties interested in corporate financial reporting. LIFO, therefore, must be considered at present an accounting practice falling outside widely accepted guidelines in many of the cases where it is used. However, this does not necessarily mean that LIFO should be eliminated; rather, it suggests that a more widely applicable procedure for recognizing the effects of inflation might well be devised.

One other important practice is in very widespread use in connection with the measurement of cost of goods sold and the amounts of inventories in the balance sheet. This is that the balance sheet amount should be stated at market prices if these are lower than cost. The transaction guideline takes ascendancy over that of matching here. It dictates that past expenditures directly related to products or services yet to be sold must be recognized as near to the original transactions as it becomes evident from external evidence that the expenditures cannot be recovered in sales prices. Thus, the transaction guideline calls for the excess of cost over market to be treated as a loss in the period of the market decline rather than in the later period when it becomes a cost of goods sold.

MEASURING OTHER COSTS AND EXPENSES

The measuring of many other costs and expenses has been dealt with earlier by way of illustrating how external factors influence corporate financial accounting, such as costs of research, development, administration, staff functions, maintenance, repairs, promotion, selling, and financing. The principal guideline for these costs is that of the transaction; i.e., they are considered costs of the period in which they arise. In general, they cannot be matched with any particular sales, nor convincingly associated more with some other year than that in which the activity took place. The method, consistently followed, is systematic.

By and large, the transaction basis of accounting for the costs in question also avoids distortion of periodic net income. This is because the functions involved continue from year to year as basic parts of the corporation's operations. They can be budgeted and controlled within limits.

To the extent that one or more of the activities *do* fluctuate in volume from year to year while revenues maintain a steadier trend, or revenues fluctuate while costs remain stable, fluctuations in corporate net income will of course ensue. Systematic and rational methods for minimizing avoidable distortions are in order. Already mentioned as examples are anticipating and providing evenly for vessel lay-up and overhaul or for relining blast furnaces. Financial accounting is and should be receptive to any other systematic and rational method for minimizing fluctuations in net income where the corporation's activities are progressing on a steadier trend than the transactions would otherwise indicate. However, it must be remembered that the further ahead the cash disbursement is from the time the resulting cost will be recorded as a deduction from revenues, invariably the greater the uncertainty as to whether the cost *does* rationally apply to the period to which it is allocated.

For most corporation costs, the expenditure is made *ahead* of the years to which it may be appropriately allocated. In other words, the amount of the cost has been established by objective evidence, and apportionment to years is the problem. During the last couple of decades, a problem has come to the fore which, while not entirely new, involves unprecedented amounts. This is the problem of measuring fair annual charges against income for expenditures *that may be made in the future*—often, the distant future. Involved are pension and income tax costs. For these items, in addition to the problem of apportioning cost among years, there is considerable uncertainty involved even in estimating the amount of the ultimate expenditures to be provided for.

MEASURING PENSION COSTS

Estimating ultimate pension payments with respect to pension credits accumulated to any given date by any given group of employees requires the making of important assumptions as to the future, such as: the pension credits that will be lost by employees before their retirement owing to separation from the corporation or death; the longevity of employees who do retire on pension; future earnings on pension funds; and the trend in future compensation. Actuarial calculations made on the basis of these assumptions are, at best, only approximations, particularly as to that portion of ultimate pension payments which is assignable to as short a period as a current year. However, the actuarial approach to a difficult measurement problem is rational and, provided subjective and capricious changes are not made in the underlying assumptions, it is systematic.

Given the actuarial calculations, however, there is still another question in connection with the corporation's total cost arising from its pension commitments. How much of the total calculated amount will become a "perpetual float" of unmatured benefits that the corporation will not be required to pay? If the corporation's net income (and therefore the stockholders' equity) is reduced by provisions for this perpetual float, which then becomes a "perpetual unmatured liability" on the balance sheet, are the stockholders' informational needs well served by the process?

The last question is directed to a corporation that does not "fund" pension benefits. What is the significance of "funding"? Obligations to individual pensioners will of course be discharged only from resources that exist at the time of the payment; the resources that existed at the time the rights to pensions arose have no relevance. If the corporation does not fund its pensions, ability to honor ultimate pension obligations will rest only on the corporation's resources at the time the obligations fall due.

The corporation can transfer its commitment to a broader base in the economy by funding—i.e., by transferring some of its cash resources today to an outside agency that invests in securities, which are claims on future resources of a number of corporations, taxing authorities, and so forth. The corporation's sacrifice in the process is the loss of resources, to the extent of the funding, for productive use in its own operations. (Questions are increasingly heard among corporate managements as to the relative advantages and disadvantages of transferring corporation resources to outside agencies to such an extent that a substantial "permanent float" of invested funds is created, on the one hand, and the funds are freed from tax on income and capital gains, on the other hand.) The act of funding, as such, would seem to have little to do with the measurement of a fair charge for pension costs in computing the corporation's periodic net income.

The measurement of the pension cost to be attributed even to current service requires assumptions about the future which are of such importance that any calculation is an approximation, at best. After pension funds or pension liabilities are accumulated beyond a certain point, there arises the question of whether further accumulations are actually a corporate cost. The assumptions as to the future required here are not unlike those involved in normal actuarial pension calculations.

When a corporation adopts a new pension plan, or changes the benefits in a present plan, further questions usually arise from the application of the formula for computing the retroactive benefits. Typically, *past* service, as well as current and future service, enter into the calculation of the future pension. For pension costs attributable to past service, what portion, if any, should be considered fair charges against current and future corporate income? This question arose on a major scale with the wholesale extension of corporate pension commitments in the late 1940's and early 1950's, and continues in debate today.

One line of argument is for a so-called "full accrual" out of present and future corporate net income of provisions for pension benefits measured by past service. This argument contends that the past could not have benefited from pension rights that did not then exist, that only the present and future can benefit from the improved employee security involved in the new or changed plan, and that the present and future must therefore bear the cost. One difficulty with this has already been mentioned, namely, whether part of a full accrual is a perpetual float and not a corporate cost at all.

Another unknown in connection with the full accrual approach is the future period over which costs attributable to past service should be provided. Some persons (mathematically oriented, no doubt) suggest that if it is the corporation's future that is benefited, that future may be infinitely long and so that portion of the total cost applicable to any one year may be, accordingly, infinitesimally small. A more usual line of reasoning is that the past-service costs should be made up over the remaining service of the employees on hand at the time the new or changed plan came into effect. This associates the costs with individuals, so to speak. Starting from this point, still another approach is to amortize the past-service costs over an arbitrary period, such as 10 years (the period commonly used for federal income tax purposes), or perhaps 25 or 40 years.

It is the transaction guideline that raises doubt as to whether periodic corporate net income should be charged for aggregate amounts greater than may reasonably be expected to be paid. However, the guideline to avoid distortions of periodic net income is also pertinent in accounting for past service costs. Whereas accumulations over a period as long as 40 years would probably make each year's portion minute in relation to net income, an accumulation over as short a period as 10 years raises a real question of distortion in comparing net incomes for the 10 years with those of the eleventh and thereafter. Shades of this problem would exist for periods of other lengths.

From the standpoint of measuring periodic net income of corporations, the characteristics of pension commitments pertinent to the determination of appropriate accounting practices vary considerably among corporations. Variations arise from the level of respective benefits and how they are accumulated, the time when plans were adopted, the extent of funding and of vesting, experience in employee turnover and in fluctuations in numbers of employees, and a number of other factors. Accordingly, only very generalized conclusions can be drawn. The conclusions offered here, which differ from those presently influencing corporate practice, are:

1. After pension commitments are entered into, each year's employment costs should include a fair charge for the amount of this year's fringe benefit. However, what is a fair charge must take into account not only this year's accumulations of benefit credits, but their modification by the ultimate corporate-requirement-to-pay.

2. The make-up of accumulations for past-service costs, which has the effect of creating a "permanent-float" liability or fund, is not a fair charge against net income measuring a corporation's current oper-

ating performance. If significant make-ups are recomended by other corporate considerations, they should be reported as unusual charges in reports to stockholders.

MEASURING FEDERAL INCOME TAX COST

It was pointed out in Chapter IV that most items of revenue and cost that enter into a computation of financial net income also enter into the determination of taxable income, but that the timing differs for some items. Where current income tax payments are substantially affected by such timing discrepancies, the problem arises as to what is a fair amount of income tax cost to be deducted currently in computing financial net income to be reported to stockholders.

Some emphasize the transaction guideline in this connection, and say that tax payments with respect to a year's operations measure that year's tax cost. They point out that accounting practices for financial and tax purposes have differed to a greater or lesser extent since income taxation began, and that any attempt to maintain a kind of running reconciliation between the two (such as showing as the tax cost of each year what it would have been if taxing authorities had accepted the corporation's financial accounting practices) would become hopelessly involved. They further argue that political, social, economic, and fiscal considerations prompt taxation authorities to change tax rates and the tax system continually, sometimes across-the-board but also often with deliberate selectivity. History teaches, they say, that a tax reduction that is selective for one reason or another cannot with confidence be expected to be "made up," with the ultimate result that all corporate taxpayers will pay the same rates on the same income.

Others emphasize the nondistortion guideline in approaching the measurement of each year's tax cost. They state that the tax laws and rules of the present are the only known guides to future taxation and that if these provide that a tax reduction now must be made up later, net income would be distorted unless the current year's actual tax payment is supplemented by a provision for the future additional tax. They also point to a loss of economic value, equivalent to the tax reduction inherent in an asset, at the time the asset is deducted from taxable income. Such loss should be recorded, they say, by a charge to income offsetting the tax reduction.

The items which raise problems of measuring the tax cost of periods may be classified in two types. The first involves non-repetitive, short-run discrepancies between financial and taxable income. Examples are: provision for a foreseen loss in an investment for financial purposes in the current year, with the loss being allowable for tax purposes only upon actual liquidation of the investment in some later year; provision in the current year for the cost of remedying mechanical defects in products in customers' hands, the necessity of the work having become known in the present year, with the costs being allowed for tax purposes only as the work is actually performed; and the deduction for tax purposes in the current year of the cost of a major research effort, which cost is carried forward for financial accounting purposes to be amortized over the next few years. For such sporadic, short-run items, the nondistortion guideline clearly prevails, and the ultimate tax impact should be, and usually is, provided for when the item enters into the financial accounting.

The second and more difficult tax cost measurement problem arises from timing discrepancies of items that recur in large numbers. The most important current example of this is depreciable property that includes a mass of items continually being turned over, and for which depreciation is computed by the straight-line method for financial purposes and by an accelerated method to determine taxable income. In these circumstances, on an item-by-item basis each property unit generates for tax purposes—in comparison with the financial accounting—more depreciation and less taxes in the early years of its life, with the opposite effect thereafter. Is financial net income distorted unless it has been charged in the earlier years with a provision for the "deferred income taxes" to be made up later?

Not necessarily. If new property units continue to replace the older ones, each providing accelerated depreciation in its earlier years, accelerated depreciation *for the mass of items* levels off to the same amount as provided by the straight-line method; the initial tax reduction becomes permanent. Had provision been made for the "pay-back" of the earlier tax reductions in later years, it would have been found that the contingency provided for did not arise. A "permanent float"—i.e., a reserve for a remote contingency—would have been provided. (Note the close parallel between accounting for tax reductions related to accelerated depreciation and accounting for pension costs. Both involve the question of departure from the transaction guideline in attributing costs to current periods which very probably will be represented by cash expenditures later when individual units are viewed, but some portion, if not all, of which become only contingencies when viewed in the mass.)

Providing for "deferred income taxes" because of depreciation differences has actually been widespread corporate practice in recent years. One of the gravest questions about corporate financial accounts that is appearing as a result is whether past net income has been reduced by amounts that time will show not to have been costs at all, or costs not of the magnitude provided for. To the extent that this has been done, net income and stockholders' equity have been reduced to create a "contingency reserve"—possibly a *remote* one—in the balance sheet.

Experience to date strongly suggests the necessity of a review of practices of providing for deferred income taxes. Some of the assumptions and calculations common in actuarial methods seem called for. Perhaps in individual cases enough, or too much provision has been made for contingent payments under assumptions of even extremely adverse future conditions. If so, then it is time to review the relative weight of the transaction and nondistortion guidelines as they apply to the measurement of corporate net incomes. It may well be that in specific cases some of the past provisions for deferred income taxes should be reversed, augmented in others, and in still others held without change.

MEASURING THE COST OF USING FIXED ASSETS

Because the useful lives of fixed assets usually extend over periods of many years, this category of advance expenditures is the best illustration of the need for accrual accounting, an area where the influence of the transaction guideline is minimal and where the influence of the nondistortion guideline is most compelling. The usual problem of amortizing fixed assets also clearly presents the fact that there is little objective evidence to measure the portion of the total costs to be matched with the revenues of any particular period, or with the period itself, for that matter. The resort has to be, then, to a systematic and rational method for measuring the period costs.

A question sometimes arises as to measurement of the periodic cost of fixed assets that are leased rather than purchased. Assume, for example, that a corporation utilizes two buildings, each with a 20-year useful life. Building A is purchased for $20 million, using proceeds from a mortgage of equal amount to be reduced evenly over the 20 years. Building B is leased for 20 years, paying level amounts of annual rent sufficient in total to provide the lessor with recovery of his investment and interest on his capital. Why, it is asked, should the corporation report higher annual costs in the earlier years for building A (depreciation plus interest cost on a declining amount of borrowed money) than in its later years, whereas its annual cost for building B is even throughout?

The transaction guideline provides most of the answer: the transactions are different. Borrowing-and-buying is a completely different business approach to obtaining the right to use property from that of leasing. One of the valid business considerations that could lead to the choice of the leasing technique, for example, is to obtain a level annual cost of property. An accounting practice that treated the leasing transaction as though some other kind of transaction had been made, would begin to suggest that the form and substance of all transactions, where corporations do things differently, should be ignored in favor of some uniform hypothetical method of doing all business. (Instances are occasionally encountered in which the leasing form disguises what is in substance an installment purchase or, when corporate shells are disregarded, a lease in form turns out to be borrow-and-buy in substance. Here, the *legal* form can and usually should be pierced to get at the substance of the *business transaction*.)

Much of the temptation to record leased assets and a related liability on the balance sheet, as though the corporation had borrowed-and-bought, appears to come from the viewpoint of a corporation's creditors. These, it is suggested, would like to see lease and mortgage commitments treated in the same manner. However, where a practice that would satisfy a creditor's interest would run afoul of the stockholders' informational need for the best measure of periodic net income, the creditor must give way to the stockholder insofar as the corporate financial report is concerned. Data on significant lease commitments should be, and is, given in footnotes, however. In any event, bankers and credit evaluation agencies are generally in a position to obtain information peculiar to their needs directly from corporations.

The Importance of Consistency
in the Measurement of Periodic Net Income

The discussion of the measurement of periodic corporate net income makes obvious the extent to which the results rely upon estimates and judgments, as well as choices from among acceptable accounting practices. The measurements could and would be chaotic if at each point where a decision were made it were made entirely subjectively, without any reference to precedents.

For example, how much of present accounts receivable will ultimately prove to be uncollectible and, therefore, should not be carried forward as an asset? In most cases, particularly where large numbers of receivables are involved, this is a matter of estimate and judgment. Suppose the corporation had developed, as a reasonable experience factor, that the bad-debt reserve should equal x per cent of accounts not yet due, y per cent of those 30 to 90 days past due, and z per cent of those more than 90 days past due. If current corporate management, without rational explanations based upon demonstrated changed conditions, varied these percentages each year by subjective judgments, the corporation's reported net incomes would become correspondingly suspect. The same point could be made with regard to the following: expenditures classified as maintenance and repairs, as distinguished from those capitalized in fixed assets as additions or betterments; the determination of overhead and other indirect costs that are included in inventory rather than treated as costs of the period in which incurred; whether revenue is to be recognized at the point of legal sale, delivery, or collection, and whether, in the case of long-term construction, as work progresses or upon its completion and acceptance; and estimates of the useful lives of fixed assets. There are many other decision points at which estimate and judgment are involved in corporate financial accounting.

Most of the corporate accounting judgments and estimates are related to repetitive transactions or events. In this regard, precedents tend to be established for both underlying rationale and appropriate method. Once so established, consistency becomes a standard: changed conditions, or errors in the prior rationale, must be *affirmatively* demonstrated to justify a departure from prior practice.

The foregoing emphasizes the role of consistency in estimates and judgments as to quantitative decisions. Consistency is of no less importance in the use of accounting practices. It will be evident from earlier discussions that for many types of transactions there are two or more acceptable accounting practices from which a corporation may choose. FIFO, LIFO, and average cost inventory methods are important examples, as are straight-line and accelerated depreciation methods. If a corporation switched freely from one year to another among such practices, the comparison of its net income among periods could be distorted and usefulness of such information to the stockholder seriously impaired. Again, the standard of consistency in using the method chosen is invoked as protection; the corporation may change from one practice to another for good cause, but if it does, it must report the change and its effect on net income to the stockholders.

Consistency in handling comparable factors underlying estimates and judgments, and in the application of accounting practices, then, provides the greatest possible assurance that any given corporation's net income over a number of years has been measured in a comparable manner. There remains the question, however, of satisfying stockholders' desires to compare the net incomes, and trends therein, of *different* corporations. If these use differing estimates, judgments, and accounting practices, can comparisons among companies be made?

The answer—for the large, mature corporations—is in the affirmative to a large extent, provided the analytical comparison is more than a simple arithmetical exercise. The comparison is facilitated by two factors: consistency, and disclosures in the balance sheet, footnotes, and supplementary information.

Most corporations deal in huge masses of similar transactions and events, each running a cycle to completion and being constantly followed by others. Most of the cycles are short: the elapsed time from acquisition of raw materials to collection of the receivable from the sale of the product made from them—from cash to cash, so to speak—is not usually long. The effects of differing estimates, judgments, and accounting practices, and even random errors, tend to cancel out among different corporations, just as estimating errors tend to do from year to year for the same corporation.

Where the operating cycles are longer (as for fixed assets), or the differences in effect of accounting practices tend to be cumulative (as for FIFO versus LIFO inventory costing in a long period of rising prices), comparisons of net incomes among corporations can be affected by differing estimates, judgments, and accounting practices. The extent to which comparisons are affected can and does differ, of course, but as a general rule it is relatively small in each year.

However, the cumulative difference over a decade or so between the balance sheet amounts of similar inventories on FIFO and LIFO bases (or depreciation on straight-line and accelerated methods) is often sizable. This makes the balance sheet disclosures about residual amounts of items to be charged against future income, and the accounting practices used for determination of these amounts, very important in appraising the relative incidence of such charges in the future. To repeat: the balance sheet thus becomes a large footnote to the income statement in that it contributes information as to how the net income of the period was determined. Most of the estimates and judgments behind the figures, too numerous to be itemized and individually not significant, are still not disclosed. However, the disclosures that *are* made, coupled with the standard of consistency, go far toward giving the knowledgeable investor the basis for making comparisons among corporations. But the exercise is not, and never will be, simple.

SUMMARY

The measurement portion of the accounting function, when applied to repetitive transactions and events, responds for the most part very directly to the external forces and influences which bear upon the corporation. The measurement is also consistent with the corporation's nature and purpose.

With respect to the four guidelines for allocating repetitive revenues and expenses to years, the matching guideline is invoked in more cases than it is applicable to, whereas the non-distortion guideline has the potential for wider application than has been recognized to date. In measuring pension and income tax costs, real costs and remote contingencies are in danger of being commingled; the distinction needs to be borne in mind by every corporation.

Consistency in the use of factors underlying estimates and judgments, and in accounting methods, is of the greatest importance in measuring a corporation's periodic net income. It also goes a long way toward providing comparability of net incomes among companies.

VI

The Measurement Process:
Other Accounting Problems

Even if the highest degree of skill and judgment is exercised in apportioning revenues and expenses over years, gains and losses will occur which are unusual in relation to any one year. Many of these can arise from the dynamics of the corporation. Other problems appear in accounting for stock dividends and splits and for treasury stock. Mergers and acquisitions present problems entirely different from those of the corporation growing from within; goodwill presents a particularly provocative question. Changes in the purchasing power of the monetary unit give rise to highly complex issues.

Measuring Unusual Gains and Losses

In every large corporation, it is normal to find in the results of each year's operations a certain amount of abnormality. Some of this arises from correction of estimates and judgments of the past, some from events of the year which were unforeseen, and some from transactions and events not in the ordinary course of the corporation's business. A partial list of items of the type under discussion follows. Some of the parenthetical comments in connection with the items suggests how they might have been handled under the accrual basis of accounting—with the benefit of perfect foresight.

131

Accounts receivable and revenues

1. Collection of an abnormally large contract price adjustment which had been in dispute or negotiation, the contract having been worked on in prior years and the price adjustment having been held in suspense. (Had it been possible to forecast accurately the final price, the effect of the adjustment would have been taken up as the contract work progressed.)

2. Bad-debt losses, established in the current year and applicable to sales in prior years, in excess of reserves by an abnormally large amount. (Had the losses been foreseen, they would have been provided for in earlier periods.)

3. Provision for bad debts, excessive in relation to past and current bad-debt experience, because such provisions are deductible for income tax purposes, as in some banks, and provisions for general reserves in savings and loan associations. (By definition, these provisions do not relate to the current period and are in the nature of provisions for contingencies but, being deductible from taxable income, they reduce the corporation's outflow of cash for income tax.)

4. A conclusion reached during a year that important amounts previously provided for bad debts are now excessive in relation to needs. (Had the ultimate facts been known, they would not have been provided originally.)

Inventories and cost of goods sold

5. Reduction of inventory cost to market by an unusually large amount owing to an unusual decline in the market. (This has happened infrequently since the early 1920's, but occasional instances may occur which deserve the description "unusual.")

6. Liquidation of inventory at a loss in other than the ordinary course of business, as when standard product lines are discontinued. (This is a change in the nature of the business—perhaps minor in relation to the whole but, nonetheless, a change—and thus merits the description "unusual.")

7. Recognition of an unusually large amount of inventory obsolescence or unsalability. (This may be due to identifiable events occurring during the year, but it may also be due to recognition during the year of the cumulative effect of developments over a period of years. If the latter, the inventory costs would not have been brought forward had the ultimate facts been known.)

8. The realization of a large profit on an abnormal liquidation of low-cost LIFO inventories during the year. (In comparison with normal experience, such profits would be unusual and nonrecurring.)

Long-term investments
9. The realization of a substantial gain or loss on disposition of a long-term business investment, or the provision for a substantial unrealized loss. (The transaction is outside the corporation's normal activity. As to the realized or unrealized losses, these may have accumulated gradually and should have been provided for currently had they been recognizable. In such a case, sudden recognition becomes a correction of a prior omission. The suddenness of recognition of a gain is more premeditated. See the discussion of this subject in Chapter III.)

Fixed assets
10. The recognition of large gains or losses on sales or abandonments of fixed assets. (Again, these are unusual events in that they are not in the corporation's ordinary course of business. Many of the gains and losses could have been obviated by different earlier provisions for depreciation and obsolescence had the ultimate disposition of the fixed assets been known all along. To that extent, the gains and losses may be considered adjustments of prior estimates of the depreciation and obsolescence provisions.)

Intangible assets
11. Large write-offs of goodwill, capitalized research and development expenses, and the like, upon concluding that such items have lost their anticipated value. (The costs involved would have been charged to expense at the time the transactions giving rise to them were entered into or amortized as they lost their value, had their future disposition been foreseen. The arguable correction of earlier judgments again is involved.)

Settlements of claims, lawsuits, and disputes
12. The recognition during the year of a large income, expense, asset, or liability as a result of a disposition of a claim, lawsuit, or dispute. (In many of these cases, the fact that a problem existed may have been known for years—as, for example, in an important income tax case—but the ultimate monetary effect was either not assessable or was estimated differently from the final outcome. Had the future been foreseeable, most of these items would have been provided for in earlier years in connection with the events that gave rise to them.)

Casualty losses
13. Losses of large amounts from fire, storm, or other catastrophe. (These relate to occurrences solely during the period but are clearly unusual in nature.)

Taking the foregoing illustrations of unusual gains and losses one by one, it is apparent that the measurement of most—once it has been determined that accounting recognition is to be given— probably presents no great difficulty. If estimates are required, their importance is probably no greater than in other phases of financial accounting. Where they are or could be the result, as seen by hindsight, of inaccurate allocations made earlier under the accrual basis of accounting, the measurement problem exists in the allocation process rather than in the unusual item when it occurs.

The foregoing comment applies to each item considered individually. However, if it is accepted that unusual gains and losses will occur,[1] there remains a measurement problem when for any one corporation such items are considered in the aggregate. The first question is whether the "unusual" items occur with sufficient frequency, or whether their net result is so small that they may be combined with the results from regular business activities—what George O. May termed a "normal amount of abnormality." For example, the net gain or loss on transactions in the portfolio of marketable securities is not often reported separately by an industrial corporation. Neither is the net result of disposing of hundreds of smaller items of fixed assets. Thus, whether items are sufficiently abnormal to be segregated from repetitive transactions is the first measurement question. It is a safe guess that most of the 397 corporations which, according to *Accounting Trends & Techniques,* did not report unusual items in 1963 did, in fact, have them to some extent. Those that reported unusual items also probably had others of smaller amount that they did not segregate.

Given unusual items whose monetary effect is sufficient to warrant segregation from the results of normal operations, the

---

1. *Accounting Trends & Techniques* reports that, in 1963, out of 600 companies 203 reported 264 items of the type under consideration (1964 edition, page 194).

next question is: Should the amount be included in the computation of the figure termed "net income for the year," excluded from it and reported separately as a special item outside net income, or reported as an adjustment of retained earnings?

This introduces a second shade of distinction between what is part of a corporation's financial trend, and what is not. That the question is asked at all is troublesome, for it places an exaggerated importance on the single figure of "net income for the year." That figure alone cannot convey the results of both repetitive operations and unusual transactions and events of a large corporation in a meaningful manner. The important consideration is that the amount of the unusual item be disclosed separately and adequately described. Whether it should be included or excluded from a measure of this year's progress involves not only perspective as to the past but an assessment of the future. The weight to be given to the statistic of "net income for the year" must be assessed by each user of the corporate financial report with this in mind. This subject will come up again in the next chapter when reporting unusual gains and losses is discussed.

Some Measurement Problems
Involving Stockholders' Equity

Continual changes in the total amount of stockholders' equity derive from the corporation's net income, gains, and losses, including the results of unusual transactions and events. The measurement of these has been discussed. Other changes arise from the payment of cash dividends and the sale of corporation stock for cash. Accounting for these presents no problems.

Measurement problems involving the amount of stockholders' equity, or subdivisions thereof, arise in connection with the issuance of corporate stock for other than cash, as well as with the acquisition of treasury stock.

SHARE DISTRIBUTIONS (STOCK DIVIDENDS
AND STOCK SPLITS)

It is a current practice in the United States to consider share distributions in the neighborhood of 25 per cent and above as stock splits, and lesser distributions as stock dividends. The corresponding current accounting practice for stock splits is to transfer from capital surplus or retained earnings to capital stock only the minimum amount necessary to satisfy legal requirements, i.e., the par or stated value of the additional shares (which is usually below the current market price). For stock dividends, the practice is to transfer from retained earnings to capital stock and capital surplus accounts an amount equal to the approximate current market value of the shares distributed. It will be observed that, in either case, the total amount of stockholders' equity is not affected—only its subdivisions.

From the corporation's standpoint, there cannot be said to be any distinction between the two classes of share distributions. For both, the corporation has increased the number of its outstanding shares without receiving additional resources. This, in itself, would suggest that it make no accounting entries at all. However, the externally imposed legal requirement necessitates the movement of the minimum legal capital into the capital stock account, but this particular requirement is no different for a stock dividend than for a stock split.

The use of current market values to account for a stock dividend would seem to ignore the separateness of the identity of the corporation and its shareholders. Current market prices are developed in trading among external parties; the corporation does not usually purport to reflect such current valuations in its accounts; yet it takes cognizance of them when it accounts for a stock dividend. To this extent, the results of transactions to which the corporation is not a party tend to be confused with the results

of those to which it is. Why, then, the current practice of accounting for stock dividends? It is believed reasonable to ascribe it to
what might be called external regulation—through positions taken
by the New York Stock Exchange and the SEC, enunciated by
pronouncements of the American Institute of Certified Public
Accountants.

The increase in corporate stock dividends a number of years
ago probably can be traced to two main factors. (1) the desire
of corporations to conserve cash for expansion, and (2) the attractiveness to stockholders of receiving without the incurrence of
income tax additional shares which could either be retained or
disposed of at capital gains rates, depending upon the cash needs
of each stockholder. The fact that any existing cash dividend rate
is usually maintained after issuance of smaller stock dividends
has the effect of a dividend increase on the old shares, which
tends to keep market prices per share from dropping, even though
there is a dilution of outstanding shares. Soundly conceived stock
dividends, then, can attain several desired objectives admirably.

The practice can be abused, however. If cash dividends are
not being paid and are a dim prospect, if continued dilution of
shares does ultimately depress the market, if the corporation's
earnings are not healthy—then the issuance of stock dividends
(at the same time that soundly based ones are being issued by
other corporations) may mislead the stockholder. He may think
that he has received something when he has received nothing.
What safeguard can be created against potential abuses? A
broad measure of a corporation's past success lies in the amount
of its retained earnings, and the current net increase therein is
an index of current success. Why not, then, require retained
earnings to be reduced by the amount of the market value of each
share issued as a "dividend"? If the amount of retained earnings
and the periodic additions thereto are sufficient to withstand such
charges, then the stock dividends are probably soundly based;

if not, then they probably should not be issued. It is believed that reasoning along these lines is the basis for the current requirement that stock dividends be accounted for at market values.

Accounting for stock dividends, then, derives from considerations sharply different from any considered before for the normally unregulated corporation. To repeat, accounting for stock dividends results from an externally imposed regulation, probably inspired by a desire to protect the stockholders of a relatively small percentage of all corporations from being misled. The requirement attempts to set up conditions, through financial accounting, under which stock dividends may be soundly issued and those in which the issuance is not so sound. It may be observed that the enforcement could have been more direct, by describing the conditions under which stock dividends could and could not be issued, with the accounting for stock dividends conforming to that of stock splits.

It may also be observed that measurement of the corporation's periodic net income is not involved in the problem of accounting for stock dividends, but rather what portion of the invested capital will be called "capital stock" and "capital surplus" and what "retained earnings." Thus, this use of an accounting practice as an enforcement tool does little to disturb the significance of that information in the financial report which is of most importance to the stockholder. Nonetheless, the use of market values to record stock dividends is so questionable as an accounting practice that it should be reconsidered, along with alternative nonaccounting restrictions on unsound stock dividends.

One footnote on terminology may be added: It would be well if the term "stock dividend" were banished from the financial lexicon. Even the most soundly based of such stock issuances do not have the significance of cash dividends. A more precise differentiating description would be "share distribution." This term is appropriate for both what are now termed "stock dividends" and "stock splits."

TREASURY STOCK

Corporations frequently use some of their resources to reacquire their own shares, usually paying the market price. They may do this in a deliberate contraction of capital, and formally retire the reacquired shares, or they may reacquire the shares with the intent of reissuing them for acquisitions, under stock option plans, employee purchase plans, and the like. When the corporation reacquires some of its shares and while it is holding them, what is their status? If it retires its shares, what is the significance of the difference between the cost thereof and the par or stated value?

The very nature of the corporation dictates that its own stock is not one of its assets. Its stock may be issued to *acquire* assets (resources), which are then put to work in the corporation's line of endeavor. But until this is done, the stock certificate is only a piece of paper. It is obvious that if every corporation's unissued stock could be construed as one of its assets, then any corporation could rise to the billion-dollar class merely by listing such stock as one of its assets. No practical questions of this type have arisen with regard to unissued stock, but they appear sometimes for reacquired stock.

When a corporation reacquires its stock, it usually gives up resources equivalent to the current market value. It has redeemed some of the external ownership and, to that extent and regardless of how minute, has effected a partial contraction, even though only temporarily. Reacquisitions of stock that is to be retired cannot be made from other than resources surplus to the corporation's business without contracting the corporation's activities. This places an effective outside limit on the practice. In addition to the practical limits on the reacquisition of stock that is to be retired, the business corporation acts of a number of states contain legal restrictions concerning transactions by a corporation in its own stock.

A small percentage of the corporations that hold treasury stock include it among their assets. Although it may be possible to pass over this practice on the grounds that the amounts involved are inconsequential, no other grounds seem persuasive for treating as an asset that which by its very nature cannot produce corporate income and is not a deferred cost chargeable to future operations. The best measurement of stockholders' equity calls for deducting the cost of treasury stock within that section of the balance sheet—a practice followed by the great majority of corporations.

When treasury stock is retired, the question frequently arises as to disposition of the difference between its cost and the amount of the par or stated value to be eliminated. If the cost is less than the par or stated value, did the corporation earn income? There seems universal agreement that, in this situation, the corporation did not; that the excess of the amount eliminated from capital stock account over cost is a "capital surplus," and not to be confused with "retained earnings."

If cost is greater than the capital stock amount, what should be the disposition of the excess? Should a charge against future earnings be involved? The latter question is not wholly illogical, for the market prices of the shares of most publicly owned corporations are higher than the reported stockholders' equity per share. The higher market price is in anticipation of future corporate earnings, perhaps equal to fifteen years' earnings at the current rate and, say, more than twice the current stockholders' equity per share. If the corporation purchases these "calls" on its future earnings, should it not, in deference to the remaining stockholders, reduce its income in the appropriate future years by the "prepaid" amounts? Otherwise, is not its future income, which the corporation has "bought," reported again as applicable to the remaining outstanding shares?

The answers to all these questions are in the negative, in practice and in theory. The questions arise from looking at the transaction from the standpoint of what has happened to and among stockholders, rather than what has happened to the corporation—and it will be remembered that the identity of the corporation is to be sharply distinguished from that of the stockholders. The *corporation* has released irrevocably some of its resources when it reacquires and retires some of its stock. None of the purchase price can be said to benefit *it* in future periods and, therefore, there is no basis for carrying the stock as an asset of the deferred-cost type for amortization against future net incomes.

Upon retirement of treasury stock, and where capital surplus exists, there are currently three methods in use for disposing of the excess of cost over the par or stated value: (1) charge the excess to retained earnings; (2) charge the excess first to capital surplus to the extent available, then to retained earnings; and (3) charge the excess to capital surplus in proportion to the number of shares being retired and the remainder to retained earnings.[2] As was observed in Chapter III, distinctions among amounts for capital stock, capital surplus, and retained earnings rest more on academic than practical considerations; therefore, for most large corporations, the choice among these methods is not of great significance to the stockholder.

The Measurement of Corporate Net Income
After Mergers and Acquisitions

Most of corporate financial accounting is developed for and applies to assets, liabilities, expenditures, and receipts relating to materials and services that the corporation acquires or sells in

---

2. This somewhat abbreviated discussion applies primarily to capital surplus associated with issuances of common stock, and ignores the fact that some capital surplus may be associated with preferred stock and other with nonstock items such as revaluations. Where such other types of capital surplus exist, different accounting treatments may be called for.

its normal business activities. Occasionally, however, the corporation acquires another going concern. Questions then arise as to the measurement of the periodic net income and the assets and liabilities of the combined enterprise. From the standpoint of the continuing corporation, the nature of the transaction and the business objectives inherent in it are likely to indicate the appropriate accounting. This is true regardless of whether assets or stock were acquired, or a merger involved, and whether stockholders of the nonsurviving corporation received cash or stock.

Some companies may be acquired for their tangible assets. For example, distilling companies have acquired others to obtain possession of the latters' inventories; companies in extractive industries have acquired others to secure their reserves of minerals in place; or a well-situated plant may be the objective of the acquisition. Other acquisitions are made to secure intangible assets: consumer preferences, such as brand names, geographical markets, or other stratified consumer allegiances; the know-how of engineering personnel, or patents or products in being; one or more able executives; and so forth. Still other acquisitions cannot be analyzed so precisely, particularly where the avowed intent is to diversify by moving into different lines of corporate activity.

When a "package" of tangible and intangible assets of a going concern is brought into a corporation, how they should be recorded should be governed primarily by what will fairly reflect the net income of the combined corporate enterprise in the future. In this connection, due regard must be had for the manner in which the surviving corporation accounts for similar items. Cash, marketable securities, receivables, and liabilities should give little difficulty. Acquired long-term business investments may have a soundly based current value higher, lower, or about the same as the amount carried on the predecessor's balance sheet; the current valuation would seem reasonable as a basis for the initial recording.

Those acquired assets which are to be amortized against income in the future—inventories, fixed assets, and deferred charges —may also be entitled to a higher or lower current valuation than the historical recorded cost of the predecessor. It is reasonable to use such current values where reliable objective measurements are obtainable. If not, unamortized cost on the predecessor's books, subject to adjustments to conform to accounting practices used by the successor for similar items, is to be preferred to judgments open to the criticism of subjective bias. The basic objective, again, is fairly reporting future net income of the combined enterprise after amortization of the amounts in question. A reasonable determination of this usually cannot be made without reference to the substance of the transaction and the circumstances surrounding it.

GOODWILL

Accounting for amounts assignable to intangibles that arise from a merger or acquisition raises complex and controversial issues. Even identifying the nature of the intangibles involved is difficult: the range may be from specific technical know-how to a brand name. The amount assignable to intangibles may be no more definite than an estimate of a specified number of future years' earnings, less amounts assigned to tangible assets. For purposes of the ensuing discussion, this is assumed to have been the best measure available and, where this is the case, the item is referred to as "goodwill," even though the value may trace to something as specific as an exclusive franchise. There are three broad possibilities of accounting for this type of goodwill: (1) plan to carry the amount in the balance sheet indefinitely, without change, as an intangible asset; (2) amortize the amount over a period of years by charges against the corporation's net income; or (3) write off the entire amount immediately as an "unusual charge," outside of the computation of the corporation's net income.

There are cases where the arguments are strong for indefinitely retaining goodwill in the balance sheet at an unchanged amount. An example would be where the underlying value is a franchise, the value of which does not diminish (and may actually increase) as time passes. Maintaining the asset avoids the reduction in stockholders' equity—the corporation's "invested capital"—which would result from its elimination. Many would question such a reduction in stockholders' equity as not useful accounting to stockholders. This would be particularly true if the corporation's retained earnings were less than the goodwill, so that eliminating the latter would throw the corporation into a deficit position.

The argument often goes in the other direction when the acquiring corporation already has goodwill of the type being acquired. Its goodwill may have arisen from past research and development or from advertising and other promotion, the cost of which was written off as incurred. A fair value of the acquiring corporation's goodwill may be many times greater than the goodwill arising from the current acquisition. At the same time, the continuing corporation's retained earnings may be ample to absorb the charge if the goodwill is written off. In these circumstances, the question is raised as to the usefulness to stockholders of continuing in the balance sheet indefinitely an amount for goodwill that is only a fraction of what could be assigned to that intangible by the continuing corporation. If the partial goodwill is retained, it is said, the balance sheet then becomes ambiguous.

Amortization of goodwill by charges against the corporation's net income over a number of years has one of two implications: the underlying values are seen to be declining or to have a terminal date; or the goodwill is seen as an undesirable item to be listed among the assets, perhaps because proof of value is difficult, so that it is thought best to eliminate it. Amortization against the corporation's net income is justified by any of several lines of reasoning. One is that the corporation has acquired and paid for future earnings; therefore, it should not report those earnings as its own but should offset against them the cost of their acquisition. Another somewhat similar but more specific argument applies where the fruits of research, development, advertising, or promotion underlie the acquired goodwill. Corporations generally charge against their income currently the costs of developing similar values of their own. Therefore, it is said, the standard of consistency suggests that a corporation's net income bear similar charges when developed values are purchased by a corporation from others. A third argument for amortizing goodwill against a corporation's net income is that, without such amortization, a corporation's management can report progressively higher periodic net income to stockholders merely by acquiring going businesses, and that even overpayments for businesses will not be revealed unless the acquired earnings are more than offset by the charge for amortization of goodwill.

The arguments against amortization of goodwill by charges to corporate net income turn largely on measurement of net income trends most useful to stockholders. If the earnings of an acquired business are expected to disappear within a few years, then there can be no objection to amortization of goodwill over those years. The corporation did not acquire a higher earning capacity and its reported actual net income should not suggest that it did. However, it is argued that the basis of most acquisitions is that the enlarged corporation's net income will be higher —indefinitely. In such a situation, it is considered unrealistic and arbitrary to report the corporation's net income as not rising to the higher plane at the time the corporation is enlarged, but rather at some future point when the amortization of goodwill happens to run out. Therefore, it is said, current reported earnings depressed by a charge for amortization of goodwill may be somewhat misleading as a starting point for the investor's assessing future earnings prospects.

The case for writing off goodwill as an "unusual charge" immediately upon acquisition stems largely from the arguments cited above against either carrying the goodwill indefinitely in the balance sheet as an asset or amortizing it against the corporation's periodic net income. Arguments for the unusual-charge treatment are strongest where the acquiring corporation has values of its own, similar to those represented by the acquired goodwill, which are not reported in its balance sheet. It is then contended that the treatment of similar items in the now enlarged enterprise should be consistent; i.e., what the former entity is not carrying forward as either an unchanging asset or one which is a deferred cost of future operations should not be carried forward for a portion of the now-enlarged entity.

The arguments against the unusual-charge treatment of goodwill are largely those in support of one of the other two methods.

It should be evident from the foregoing discussion that there is no open-and-shut case for any one treatment of goodwill. Stockholder purposes may well be better served by use of one of the methods in one instance and a different method in quite a different situation. However, as a general proposition, it would seem that amortizing goodwill is of questionable usefulness to stockholders of most large, publicly owned corporations where in essence the goodwill is a prepayment for a portion of the anticipated future earnings of an acquired company. It would seem clearer corporate reporting to eliminate such amounts as soon as they arise, so that subsequent combined net income reflects the results of combined operations. The sudden increase in earnings of the surviving corporation then reflects the fact of a combination. At the same time, there would be eliminated from the balance sheet an amount for intangibles which is incomplete and which, in any event, balance sheets do not purport to evaluate. However, if this course is followed, stockholders are then in need of a further item of information: a comparison of subsequent combined net incomes with the combined net income record of the constituent businesses prior to the merger or acquisition. This information can best be provided by restating historical data. The matter is discussed in the next chapter in connection with financial reporting.

Mergers and acquisitions have been discussed above without reference to whether the consideration given up by the continuing corporation was cash or stock. Insofar as accounting for future periodic net income of the enlarged enterprise is concerned, there seems no basis for making a distinction. If the acquiring corporation gives its own stock in exchange for a business, then it has given up none of its resources (its own stock not being one of its assets). The minimum amount the corporation is required to assign to the capital stock issued is its par or stated value. Over that amount, the valuation of the stock issued should derive from the tangible assets acquired by the corporation. When stock is issued, there is not the same need to arrive at a residual figure for goodwill as when cash is involved, and no useful stockholder purpose would seem to be served by doing so. This would apply even where the stock issued is treasury stock purchased at market prices; again, there would seem to be no useful purpose nor logical reason for placing the accounting for assets acquired with it on a different basis from those acquired with stock hitherto unissued.

In mergers (the acquiring corporation having issued stock), the question may arise as to whether any part of the retained earnings of the acquired corporation may be brought into and reported as retained earnings of the combined enterprise. As indicated earlier, the distinctions between retained earnings and other elements of stockholders' equity are academic for most large, publicly owned corporations; the entire amount is "invested capital" as a practical matter. However, the importance of the distinction between the elements of stockholders' equity is inversely proportional to the relative amount of retained earnings; the smaller the amount of retained earnings, the more important it is to know its size. In any event, where stockholders of two corporations have "pooled interests" in a continuing corporation in which they become common owners, there seems little basis in reality or logic for considering that the retained earnings of the combined enterprise are confined to those formerly owned by one of the sets of stockholders, and that the retained earnings of the other should become dedicated "capital." On the contrary, it would seem much more rational to view the "pooling" completely as such, extending to retained earnings as well as to other items in the balance sheet. Current practice largely follows this view.

Measurement Implications of Changes in Purchasing Power of the Monetary Unit

It has already been pointed out that corporate financial accounting in the United States ignores fluctuations in the purchasing power of the dollar. Historical costs are measured with historical dollars. No attempt is made to translate the cost arising from an expenditure made years ago into equivalent dollars of the same purchasing power today. The important measurement implication of this financial accounting practice is that dollar amounts of various items in the income statement are in terms of varying purchasing power equivalents.

The implicit assumption that the purchasing power of the monetary unit is stable is an area where modern corporate financial accounting has not responded in a realistic way to external forces and influences. Whether or not this was their justification for the practices, income taxation authorities and some corporations in reports to stockholders have, in effect, adjusted for price level changes in the two important deferred-cost items of inventories and fixed assets by authorizing the use of, respectively, the LIFO and accelerated depreciation methods. However, these may be considered expedients in comparison with an overt recognition that the monetary unit is sufficiently unstable for corporate financial accounting to adjust to the fact.

The goal should be that the various items of revenue and expense in each annual income statement are reasonably expressed in terms of the purchasing power of current dollars. This will require the conversion of the historical dollar cost of deferred-cost assets to the current-dollar equivalent, with a concomitant increase in a special category of stockholders' equity. Amortization of these assets (after a rising price level) will be correspondingly higher and the reported periodic net income correspondingly lower. This increased amortization may be offset or increased, depending upon the interplay of the amounts of monetary assets subject to inflation loss and monetary liabilities that provide a hedge against inflation.

The impact of inflation varies with each corporation, and therefore the mechanics of the adjustment must vary accordingly. However, it is clear that corporate financial accounting should not continue to assume that the monetary unit is stable.

Summary

Within the income statement, unusual gains and losses need to be segregated from the results of more normal repetitive transactions and events affecting the corporation. This need is widely recognized.

Accounting for stock splits, stock dividends, and treasury

stock needs to be put in perspective. However, most of the questions involve the relative amounts of capital surplus and retained earnings, a distinction of little importance to the stockholder of most large corporations.

Accounting treatment of goodwill needs to be seriously reconsidered. The arguments are strong that goodwill attributable solely to the purchase of future earnings expectations should not be carried forward in the balance sheet of most large, publicly owned corporations, and that it should not be amortized against the corporation's periodic net income. Instead, it should be eliminated as an "unusual charge" when it arises. However, eliminations of such goodwill should be accompanied by appropriate adjustments in historical summaries; this problem will be dealt with in the next chapter.

An assumption underlying present-day corporate financial accounting—that the United States dollar is stable in purchasing power—is not valid. This is an environmental force to which corporate financial accounting has *not* adjusted.

VII

The Communication Process: Financial Reporting

If the corporation's progress in a year cannot be neatly capsuled into one or two statistics; if judgment and estimate have entered importantly into arriving at the reported financial position and results of operations; if there is overemphasis on the current year in relation to the longer term—then full and fair disclosure of facts, judgments, and estimates is in the best interests of both stockholder and management. In particular, it seems that the current year's results have been overemphasized and that the longer-term historical summaries should be developed into a prime disclosure vehicle. The rise of the sophisticated investor and financial analyst calls for a supplement offered for their purposes.

The principle of full and fair disclosure to stockholders has been embraced by a high and steadily increasing percentage of modern corporate managements, and it has been adopted as national policy. This principle is the overriding tenet of the communication aspect of the accounting function.

That full and fair disclosure is a sound principle is demonstrated from whatever aspect it is viewed. The complexity of the corporation suggests that its progress and status cannot be adequately depicted by a few figures standing alone. Inescapable estimates and judgments lie behind many of the figures. Con-

151

tingencies exist which defy accurate measurement. Information about these estimates, judgments, and contingencies is useful to the stockholder, enabling him to put the bare figures in better perspective both in reviewing the corporation's own past history and in making comparisons among corporations. From management's standpoint, full and fair disclosure passes some of the responsibility for assessing the significance of judgments, estimates, and contingencies to the users of financial statements.

Details of the information currently being furnished to stockholders in annual reports can be found in such reference works as *Accounting Trends & Techniques*, published annually for the last eighteen years by the American Institute of Certified Public Accountants, New York. It classifies and summarizes the types of financial information contained in 600 reports of industrial and commercial corporations. Another reference is Paul Grady's *Inventory of Generally Accepted Accounting Principles* (American Institute of Certified Public Accountants, New York, 1965). This prodigious work deals extensively with matters of disclosure, though more in terms of the "what ought" than the "what is" of *Accounting Trends & Techniques*.

From these and other sources, plus a cover-to-cover review of the annual reports of a hundred large industrial corporations, it is clear that precedent can be found for disclosure of about any and every type of financial information imaginable. The extent of disclosure is generally great; that many managements have gone considerably beyond minimums suggested by convention or prescribed by rule is evident from a review of only a small number of reports. However, the scope and detail of disclosures are uneven among corporations, even among those in a fairly well-defined industry.

Discussion and Evaluation of Current Disclosure Practices

The following discussion of current disclosures in corporate financial reports may be divided into six subject areas of major interest to the stockholder: (1) defining the enterprise for financial statement purposes (consolidation practice); (2) repetitive revenues and expenses; (3) unusual gains and losses; (4) contingencies; (5) stockholders' equity; and (6) corporate liquidity. It will be noted that these also were the subject of the earlier discussions of environmental forces and measurement problems.

DEFINING THE ENTERPRISE FOR FINANCIAL STATEMENT PURPOSES (CONSOLIDATION PRACTICE)

Most large corporate enterprises consist of the parent corporation and a number of subsidiary (more than 50 per cent owned) and affiliated (50 per cent or less owned) corporations. From the standpoint of the parent alone, each of these is one of its "investments." Some of the subsidiaries are in lines of business integrated with or similar to those of other members of the corporate family; others differ radically. Some are domestic; others, foreign. Some are under close centralized control; others operate virtually independently.

Experience has demonstrated that the most useful primary financial information to the stockholder is generally that provided by consolidated financial statements of the whole enterprise—statements in which intrafamily corporate lines are ignored, and position and results are presented as though one unit. However, in both Chapters II and III it was suggested that this rule-of-thumb should by no means be followed blindly—that circumstances can also strongly suggest exclusions of subsidiaries from consolidations, and that the closeness in significance of a dollar of a subsidiary's earnings to one of a parent is a key question of judgment. For this reason, it is wise for management to disclose, and useful to the stockholder to know, both what is within a consolidation and what has been excluded from it.

Inclusions and exclusions from consolidations can be ascertained from most annual reports. In some, a direct statement of the principles of consolidation is made in a footnote. In others, a combination of the heading on the financial statements ("XYZ Corporation and wholly owned subsidiaries"), plus the captions of investments in the consolidated balance sheet ("domestic subsidiaries less than 100 per cent owned"; "foreign subsidiaries"), tell a clear story to the closer observer. In many cases, the names of the subsidiaries included and excluded, their location, and the nature of their business can be ascertained from financial statements, footnotes, management's commentary, or the tables of locations, products, and corporate entities included in most reports.

Subsidiaries excluded from a consolidation automatically become an "investment" in the consolidated balance sheet. As such, they are to be classed with investments in affiliated companies and other business investments from the standpoint of disclosures of information about them. The key question about this whole group is whether and to what extent there exists measurable unrealized appreciation or depreciation that has not yet been recognized in reporting corporate income, both for the year and cumulative to date. Further, if any such elements have been recognized, the extent of write-downs (through provisions for losses) or write-ups (as when undistributed earnings of the subsidiaries are reflected currently in consolidated net earnings) is useful information. The point is that such unrealized appreciation or depreciation usually is progressive over the years, rather than occurring suddenly. Current disclosure of such developments can mitigate the otherwise startling effect on the stockholder of a sudden *realized* gain or loss from disposition of investments appearing in the income or retained-earnings statement.

It might be added that disclosure is no substitute for providing out of income for depreciation in investments where a reasonable case cannot be made that it is temporary. As to unrealized appreciation, the burden of justification as to its recognition in corporate income should go the other way, but it can be sustained for the undistributed earnings of a subsidiary operating under stable conditions and sometimes in other cases where plans for early realization are relatively firm.

A somewhat different type of reporting problem exists where an enterprise consists of two or more segments in distinctly different lines of business, or under differing geographical influences, or otherwise clearly subject to different trends and risks. Whether such an enterprise is consolidated or not, and even whether it consists of divisions rather than subsidiaries, careful consideration needs to be given to the disclosure of available, pertinent information about each important segment. Thus, disclosures concerning foreign assets and operations—sometimes by supplementary complete financial statements, sometimes by highlight summaries—are commonly found and are important information to the stockholder. The same is true of insurance or banking subsidiaries of industrial parents. These are usually not consolidated; the mere combination of their figures with those of radically different businesses would make the whole less meaningful.

Some corporations segment their operations by major product lines and disclose the sales volume of each. A very few report in general or specific terms about net incomes of one or more of these lines. Any information of this type is highly useful to the stockholder. On the other hand, disclosures that would lose or reduce a competitive advantage would not be in the stockholder's overall best interest and, of course, should be avoided.

However, this point needs to be realistically evaluated in terms of what competitors already know. There are other cases in which operations are so interrelated that the segmenting would require the making of such major arbitrary assumptions that the meaningfulness of the results would be dubious. In still other cases, however, reluctance to make disclosures stems solely from the management's embarrassment that downward trends are hidden in the whole; in these cases, the health of the entire corporation-stockholder-society relationship calls for the disclosure.

This reporting of meaningful data about major separable segments of the entire enterprise deserves careful consideration by all corporate managements. Its importance has been highlighted by the extensive merger and acquisition movement in recent years, particularly in those cases where the objective was to diversify. The clearest case will usually be found for reporting segmented revenues. Whereas some costs can also be segregated, in the usual case it is questionable whether the compartmentalization should be carried to the point of attempting to show the contribution of each segment to the consolidated net income. However, with effort, many of these segregations could be improved for internal use and possibly for eventual dissemination to external parties.

In the attempt to define and describe the financial aspects of an enterprise within the confines of conventional financial statements, even the best judgmental solution leaves questions. If subsidiaries are not consolidated, why not? What useful information can be furnished regarding them? For operations that are consolidated, whether in subsidiaries or divisions, to what extent does the consolidation represent a confusing mixture? Given the total picture, how much information about its major components needs to be known to make it most meaningful? The net result is that defining and describing the enterprise in financial terms becomes, not a black-and-white question of consolidation or

nonconsolidation of subsidiaries, but a question of supplement-
ing the information in whatever financial statements are decided
upon for the "enterprise" by describing the nuances in gray.
Management's *reasons* for inclusion or exclusion of components
from consolidation are largely undisclosed at the moment. Disclosing them would be useful to investors, and would improve
management-stockholder understanding.

DISCLOSURES ABOUT RECURRING
REVENUES AND EXPENSES

The recurring revenues and expenses in mind here are those
which make up the main body of the corporation's income statement. In fact, they are the entire income statement unless there
exist unusual gains or losses. Disclosure questions about recurring revenues and expenses fall into two groups: itemization, and
allocation practices.

Itemization. The separately stated items of revenues and
expenses in the large corporation's income statement rarely number more than a dozen and sometimes are less than half that number. These are the result of grouping underlying accounts and
subaccounts, which together may number in the hundreds or
even thousands in the various "books" within the enterprise.
How much detail to present to stockholders is an important question of judgment, quite aside from the matter of disclosing competitive advantages and disadvantages. Whatever detail is chosen
will usually be considered too little by some and too much by
others; perhaps the most generally criticized financial statements,
for example, were the old-style ones of the railroads, in which
page after page of figures were given just as they came from the
corporation's books and as reported to the ICC.

One of two approaches to itemization of expenses is used by
most corporations. These might be termed the "functional" and

the "natural" expense. Thus, most income statements resemble one of these two:

Functional	*Natural expense*
Revenues (one or more items)	Revenues (one or more items)
Less–Cost of goods sold	
Gross profit	Expenses:
	Employment
Expenses:	Materials and services purchased
Selling, general, and administra-	Cost of facilities (depreciation)
tive	Taxes, other than federal income
Depreciation	tax
Interest	Interest
Federal income tax	Federal income tax
Net income for the year	Net income for the year

It will be noted that the essential difference between the two is that in the second grouping, employment, purchase, and certain tax costs are shown as such, rather than included in amounts of cost of goods sold, or in selling, general, and administrative expenses.

Which is the more useful disclosure? The argument is heard that the amounts of cost of goods sold and of gross profit constitute highly significant information, which the natural expense approach does not disclose. This is undoubtedly true for corporations whose activities are essentially confined to merchandising, as well as manufacturing corporations that are neither in more than one business nor sell at different distribution levels. The two figures can be a conglomeration in which even the trends have little significance for a corporation that sells at manufacturer's, wholesale, and retail levels; or one with a variety of products having different distribution systems and gross margins; or one with significant foreign as well as domestic operations. For corporations having some of these characteristics, on the other hand, the trends among employment, purchase, and tax costs in relation to sales can differ, and this can be meaningful.

Some corporations disclose their expenses on both bases, one in the income statement and the other elsewhere in the annual report. This elaboration is to be applauded, particularly where the trend in consolidated gross profit is considered to have some significance, even if slight. However, the increase in the complexity and diversity of corporations during the last several decades seems a likely prospect for the future. For many such corporations, the natural expense breakdown would seem more meaningful than the functional one. A conclusion in this matter which is valid for all corporations cannot, of course, be reached. However, companies within well-defined industries should find it possible to establish a consensus as to which form is superior to the other for their situation.

The discussion of itemization so far has been confined to minimum disclosure in the income statement itself. Many income statements are considerably more detailed than has been suggested. In addition, further elaboration of items of income and expense can be found in footnotes, supplementary tables, management's commentary, and charts.[1] Instances of numerous specific disclosures somewhere in the annual report can be found in the AICPA's *Accounting Trends & Techniques*; examples are:

Revenues
  Breakdown by product groups or geographical areas
  Quantities shipped; unfilled orders

Employment costs
  Wages and salaries
  Social security taxes
  Pension and retirement costs
  Group life, hospitalization, and sick leave costs
  Other employee benefits
  Number of employees

---

1. Most of these disclosures go considerably beyond any minimums prescribed to the corporation by external authority. That this must and always will be so is the nature of things. Requirements of centralized bodies must deal with the lowest common denominator of the units covered. Managements that are progressive in recognizing the value of disclosure in corporation-stockholder-society relations will always be ahead of any centrally imposed minimum requirements.

    Cost of facilities
      Depreciation
      Rental expense
      Maintenance and repairs
    Research and development costs
    State, local, and miscellaneous taxes
    Charitable contributions

Each of recent years has seen more itemization of revenues and expenses in corporate annual reports as a group. The additional disclosures would seem to center on items the changes in which are of concern to management and which they feel that stockholders also should study. Rising employment costs, particularly the growing prominence of fringe benefits, would be an example, as would the high postwar tax burden. The trend toward renting rather than owning facilities, as well as the increasing relative importance of facilities in many corporations' operations—resulting from both technological developments and a flight from high-cost labor—undoubtedly underlie disclosures in this area. The few but increasing disclosures of the amount of research and development expenses relate to the major upsurge of emphasis on research and development. Most corporations are affected and deeply involved. The costs of these attempts to pierce the future are considered significant and useful information by most sophisticated stockholders and analysts. So are the *results* of R&D in new products and services, most of which seem to be reported to stockholders in management's commentaries.

Trends of the future will undoubtedly render disclosures of some of these items of less significance and emphasize others. As long as corporate activities remain dynamic, that itemization of revenues and expenses which is most useful to stockholders will not remain static.

Allocation practices. The second grouping of disclosure questions concerning recurring revenues and expenses has to do with allocations. Involved are those receipts and disbursements made in one year but allocable to two or more other years. The most important of these items relate to fixed assets, inventories, R&D and other intangibles, pensions, and deferred taxes.

Since judgment and estimate enter into most allocations, it is useful to the stockholder to know as much about the allocations as it is practicable to present in an annual report. This is particularly pertinent when the stockholder or his analyst attempts to make comparisons among companies. Information about allocations will usually fall into one or more of these categories: (1) the original amount to be allocated; (2) the amount allocated to the current year; (3) the cumulative amount allocated to date; (4) the amount remaining to be allocated; and (5) an explanation of the apportionment practice adopted.

Disclosures of original amounts to be allocated are illustrated by the cost of fixed assets and the original amount of intangible assets.

Amounts allocated to the current year are invariably shown for depreciation of fixed assets, and often for amortization of intangibles, provision for loss in value of investments, and accruals for deferred taxes and for pensions.

Cumulative amounts allocated to date are illustrated by balance sheet disclosures of accumulated depreciation of fixed assets and amortization of intangibles, the provision for bad debts, valuation provisions for investments, and reserves for pensions, deferred taxes, and self-insurance. The total amount in a separate pension fund may be an indication of cumulative allocations, although this is usually a mixture of original contributions and fund earnings less payments to date.

Disclosures of amounts remaining to be allocated would include: the unamortized balances of fixed assets or intangibles; inventories; prepaid and deferred costs, including R&D; and the unprovided-for actuarial calculation of pension commitments.

Allocation practices adopted will be found described or implied, in balance sheet captions, in footnotes or management's commentaries, and in the fact that an allocation appears in the income statement or the balance sheet. Thus, the description of inventory amounts as "at the lower of cost (on the FIFO method) or market" describes an allocation practice. The fact that marketable securities are stated at market prices, below cost, implies that the practice has been adopted of charging income currently with unrealized depreciation. Narrative explanations of practices adopted for depreciation, amortization, federal income taxes, pensions, and other subjects important to a particular corporation, are frequently found.

Corporate disclosures regarding allocation practices are generally impressive, but they are uneven. It is probable that too much emphasis has been placed on reaching a conclusion that is sound in a particular corporation's circumstances; this should be given the top priority, of course, but not enough consideration has been given by many corporations to explaining the nature and extent of the judgments and estimates involved.

In the light of the growing trend of comparisons among companies which are being made by increasingly sophisticated analysts and investors, disclosure regarding allocation practices is probably the area most susceptible to improvement in corporate financial reporting. For each significant category of revenue and expense where the period or periods for the allocation are arguable, consideration should be given to whether disclosure is sufficient as to amounts involved, practices adopted, and reasons for the choice of practices.

DISCLOSURES REGARDING UNUSUAL GAINS AND LOSSES

In the preceding chapter on measurement, it was brought out that, no matter how carefully judgment is exercised and estimates are made in arriving at periodic net income, it is clear that corporations must still occasionally report, as a part of the year's accounting, unusual gains and losses. It was noted there that in

1963, about one-third of 600 companies disclosed items of this type. Among those items, adjustments resulting from the sale or disposal of fixed assets appeared three times as often as the next most frequent item.

Many of the so-called unusual gains and losses are reported as such only because of the relatively short portion of the corporation's existence to which they are ascribed—one year. If the corporation's income statement covered a 10-year or 20-year period, the chances are that most of the items would cease to be considered unusual. They would appear less material in relation to the remainder of the corporation's results, for one thing. For another, they would become more of a correction of the result of judgment and estimate reflected elsewhere in the income statement.

In the disposal of fixed assets, for example, the proceeds from sale of scrap is precisely the salvage value. An *estimated* salvage value had been used from inception in setting depreciation rates. The beginning and ending of the cycle for most fixed assets would have been wholly or largely run in the 10- or-20-year income statement, and the depreciation could be calculated more precisely. The shorter the period of time for measuring a corporation's income, then, the more likely that transactions or events will transpire which must be considered unusual in relation to that period.

The principal reporting precept regarding unusual gains and losses is that they be disclosed. Whether they are considered to be fairly includable, or fairly excludable, in arriving at the amount designated as "net income for the year," it is important to stockholders that the description and amount be reported separately from the results of recurring, repetitive operations. If they are obscured by being merged into what appear to be the results of the corporation's continuous activities, the apparent trend in the latter may not be valid.

There is a certain amount of confusion at the present time on how to report unusual items. Should they be included in the computation of the corporation's net income for the year? Should they be reported as "special items" immediately below that figure? Should they be reported as charges or credits directly to retained earnings, to "surplus"? All three treatments will be found in current annual reports, thus:

Charge Included in Computing Net Income

	(THOUSANDS)
. . .	. . . . .
. . .	. . . . .
Loss on disposal of facilities	$ 400
NET INCOME FOR THE YEAR	$ 5,000
Retained earnings at beginning of year	25,000
Dividends paid	(2,500)
Retained earnings at end of year	$27,500

"Special Charge" After Arriving at Net Income

. . .	. . . . .
. . .	. . . . .
NET INCOME FOR THE YEAR	$ 5,000
Special charge—Loss on disposal of facilities (less related tax effect)	2,500
Net income less special charge	$ 2,500
Retained earnings at beginning of year	25,000
Dividends paid	(2,500)
Retained earnings at end of year	$25,000

Charge Directly to Retained Earnings

. . .	. . . . .
. . .	. . . . .
NET INCOME FOR THE YEAR	$ 5,000
Retained earnings at beginning of year	25,000
Loss on disposal of facilities (less related tax effect)	(6,000)
Dividends paid	(2,500)
Retained earnings at end of year	$21,500

In the three illustrations above, as the size of the unusual item becomes larger, the farther away from the net income figure it is placed. This is often the practical test in deciding on the placement. However, in reality, some difficult questions arise when differences in the ratio of the unusual item to net income are considerably less than in the above illustrations. The confusion of investors can be compounded by management's commentaries on the year's results if some speak of the net income figure without mentioning the unusual item, others mention them both in the same breath, and still others talk only about the result after combining the two.

The fact that there are very few unusual charges or credits which, with the benefit of full hindsight, could not have been allocated to the corporation's income in one or more periods suggests that most of them belong in the computation of long-term corporation income, that it is the short time period that causes the difficulty. To some this argues for an "all-inclusive" income statement, wherein the results of the year's recurring transactions and its extraordinary items are combined to arrive at "net income for the year" regardless of how much fluctuation in that figure is the result. The rationale is that, since the unusual items belong in the net income at *some* point, the only logical time for their inclusion is when events giving rise to their recognition occur.

Others respond that the all-inclusive income statement is less useful to stockholders than one emphasizing "current operating performance." These say that unusual items almost invariably are liquidations of the past, and that the historical trend most useful to the stockholder as he attempts to gauge the future is that of the corporation's recurring, continuing business activities—the current operating performance. They think that unusual items should be omitted from the computation of net income for the year.

Those supporting the all-inclusive approach rejoin that a corporation's current operating performance can be made to look better than it is if provisions for losses, obsolescence, and the like can be avoided currently so that they accumulate to the point where, when recognized, they are "unusual."

So the argument goes. It probably derives from the financial community's emphasis on the one statistic of net income per share to describe a corporation's progress. If there is to be only one statistic, then what is included and excluded in arriving at it becomes overwhelmingly important. *However, in the best interests of stockholders, it is time to attack this oversimplification frontally. It is time to emphasize to stockholders that some results of a corporation's activities can be reliably measured over a year's time. Other results will "bunch up" no matter how good the judgment and estimate and become "unusual" items for a year standing alone, but more usual when viewed over a longer period. Both cannot be fitted into the same mold.*

The best solution would perhaps be a two-part income statement whenever a corporation has unusual items. The first part would report the results of repetitive transactions—recurring activities—the current operating performance, less applicable federal income taxes. The second part would give descriptions and amounts for each item considered unusual for the year, with the federal income tax effect shown. There would be no charges or credits directly to retained earnings other than those essentially capital in nature, such as charges for stock distributions. The resulting income statement gives latitude for segregating, and reporting as unusual, items and amounts that result from transactions or events that are not extraordinary except as to their infrequency or size; e.g., the sale of a bargain purchase of inventory in bulk, a change in method of measuring obsolescence in inventory, and settlements of prior years' federal income taxes which are unusually large. A skeleton of such a statement follows:

XYZ CORPORATION AND SUBSIDIARIES

Consolidated Income Statement
for the Years 1964 and 1963
(THOUSANDS OF DOLLARS)

	1964	1963
Current Performance		
Revenues	$66,000	$63,000
Expenses:		
Materials and services	$30,000	$29,000
Employment costs	23,000	22,300
Depreciation	3,500	3,400
Interest	400	400
Federal income taxes	4,500	4,000
	$61,400	$59,100
NET OPERATING INCOME FOR THE YEAR (per share of common stock: $1.15 and $.98)	$ 4,600	$ 3,900
Unusual Credits and (Charges)		
Loss on abandonment of plant		$(1,000)
Gain on sale of investment	$ 750	
Settlement of lawsuit	(500)	
Federal income tax effect of foregoing	100	500
Net unusual credits and (charges)	$ 350	$ (500)
NET RESULT FOR THE YEAR (per share of common stock: $1.24 and $.85)	$ 4,950	$ 3,400
Dividends paid	2,600	2,000
Amount added to retained earnings	$ 2,350	$ 1,400
Retained earnings at beginning of year	24,400	23,000
Retained earnings at end of year	$26,750	$24,400

A skeptic as to management's freedom from bias would argue that the foregoing would permit management to rationalize most gains into the current performance section and most losses into the unusual transaction category. There can be, however, two restraints on this: first, this recommendation should be considered an integral part of one made subsequently that historical summaries of net income cover at least 10 years, and that the unusual charges and credits be summarized separately therein. This seems a long enough period to demonstrate whether items termed unusual are actually such or are sporadic corrections of the measurement of current performance. The second restraint arises from the fact that most managements look to next year while reporting on the current one; they know that an inflated operating net income this year will make the succeeding year suffer by comparison—to management's discomfort.

The two-part income statement would be essentially a clarification and formalization of information about unusual gains and losses largely disclosed now, but in divergent ways. This form of disclosure most fairly reconciles stockholder informational needs with the problem of measuring the corporation's financial progress resulting from (1) continuously repetitive transactions and events and (2) those which are sporadic.

DISCLOSURES REGARDING CONTINGENCIES

Disclosures regarding contingencies are a further recognition that the best judgment or estimate cannot ever assay the future with assurance. What will be the ultimate outcome of important pending litigation? How will an important tax controversy be resolved? What will be the future cost of make-good work under existing guaranties or warranties?

It is the first obligation of good financial accounting to compute current income after including in the computation the best estimate of revenues and costs, belonging to the past or present, including those that will be accurately measured only by future events. Beyond that, however, it is both useful to stockholders and safest for management to disclose the nature and, if possible, the dimensions of contingencies. This is frequently done in footnotes or in management's commentary. *Accounting Trends & Techniques* (1964 ed., p. 139) reports that in 1963 some 260 of the 600 companies reported 404 items of contingent liabilities.

There is some reason to believe that the thinking about the place of contingencies in financial accounting and reporting has become oversimplified in recent years. There seems a tendency, particularly with regard to contingent future payments, to convert the contingencies into actual liabilities, measurable now. Deferred income taxes and pensions, discussed in the preceding chapter, are cases in point. Some portions of these are contingencies; yet they are recorded on corporations' books as actual current costs and as a kind of liability-equity on the balance sheet. At the same time, claims in litigation and asserted but disputed deficiencies in income taxes are, usually rightly, relegated to footnotes.

Every corporation at some time or another is surrounded by contingencies that may have financial consequences. They are an inescapable part of the corporation's operations and progress. Contingencies that can reasonably be reduced to assets or liabilities in financial reports cease to merit the description; those that cannot are properly the subject of description and discussion in footnotes and commentary. That they are not reduced to amounts entered in the financial statements should not be considered a failure of the accounting function, but the wisest application of it.

Most discussions of contingencies center on contingent *liabilities*, which (as opposed to "commitments") are the balance sheet aspect of unrealized expenses and losses. Not so much is heard of contingent *assets*, i.e., unrealized gains or appreciation. Perhaps because of this, one occasionally hears the recommendation that unrealized appreciation be counted among the corporation's assets and that current increments therein be included in corporate net income. This possibility was discussed and dismissed earlier as not being feasible and, in any event, not of probable usefulness to the stockholder.

But this does not mean that disclosure of such information as exists about unrealized appreciation and contingent assets should not be as useful to the stockholder as that about contingent costs and liabilities. This is already done, in effect, when a corporation reports the excess of market price of securities over their cost, or when it reports the equity underlying the investment in a subsidiary or associated company in comparison with its cost.

Opportunities for broadening this approach should be pursued. The growing practice of reporting, in quantities, estimates of recoverable minerals in place or uncut timber, for example, is along these lines. There is often an understandable fear on the part of managements that any discussion of contingent assets will buoy stockholder hopes more than information at hand warrants. However, where a contingency seems real enough to talk about at all, it is usually possible to shape comments that will put it in proper perspective.

By far the strongest candidate for disclosure is the appreciation or contingent asset that appears near to realization. Failure to disclose this gives rise to accusations of "insider" advantages in relation to outside stockholders. On the other hand, the negotiations leading to many of these realized gains are conducted in strict secrecy for good reasons. These may include the desire not to disturb affected employees if the sale of a portion of the business does *not* go through, or not to anticipate the signing of a binding agreement under which the corporation receives a substantial sum in settlement of a claim, for fear that a "strike suit" against the payor would postpone or upset the settlement. What can be urged about instances where the discovery or realization of important contingent assets seems a good near-term prospect is (1) that those involved keep constantly in mind the importance of the earliest possible disclosures to stockholders, (2) that selective disclosures among stockholders or others be carefully guarded against, and (3) that those with inside information not use their privileged communication for private gain.

INCOME TAX STATUS OF ASSETS AND LIABILITIES

Because the federal income tax rate is high, an important attribute of an asset or liability in the balance sheet is its income tax status. There are these presumptions about the major balance sheet items:

1. That marketable securities, receivables, and long-term investments can be converted into cash at their book value without incurring liability for payment of income tax; i.e., "book basis" and "tax basis" are the same.

2. That inventories, unamortized fixed assets, deferred charges, prepaid expenses, and deferred research and development costs will be a future deduction in computing taxable income, as they will be in computing financial income.

3. That obligations arising from accrued expenses gave rise to a tax deduction when they were created. Therefore, there will not be a tax deduction when the obligations are liquidated.

Any contradiction of the foregoing presumptions involving an important amount should be carefully considered for disclosure. This applies particularly to the unamortized balance of fixed assets, where large amounts are usually involved and historical differences between depreciation deductions for tax and financial purposes may have created discrepancies with important potential financial consequences.

DISCLOSURES ABOUT STOCKHOLDERS' EQUITY

Disclosures regarding stockholders' equity by itself are not very detailed, and need not be. The elements of capital stock, capital surplus (sometimes these two are combined), and retained earnings are itemized in a rather standardized format; in addition, the number of shares authorized and outstanding is stated.

One of the more significant disclosures pertains to the amount of retained earnings that cannot be used for the payment of dividends, the restriction arising under debt, preferred stock, or other agreements. According to *Accounting Trends & Techniques,* in 1963, two-thirds of the 600 companies reported such restrictions. A review of 100 of the 500 large industrial corporations listed by *Fortune* reveals that a slightly lower percentage, 59 per cent, reported dividend restrictions. However, in relation to current dividend payments, the practical effect of the restrictions for the hundred corporations may be suggested thus:

Number of years' current dividend requirements covered by unrestricted retained earnings	*Number of companies*
Under 1	2
1.0-1.9	7
2.0-2.9	5
3.0-3.9	7
4.0-4.9	9
5.0-9.9	12
Over 10	9
Restriction on other bases	2
No dividends paid	6
	59

Few corporations continue to pay dividends—certainly not dividends on common stock—long after they begin to exceed current income. For this reason, and also because about one-half of the above companies had unrestricted retained earnings sufficient to continue dividends for four or more years even with break-even operations, disclosures of restrictions on retained earnings are more of technical and psychological, than of practical, significance in most cases. Current net earnings plus the availability of cash continue to be the best index of capacity and willingness of a corporation to pay dividends, which emphasizes again that the cumulative amount of a corporation's retained earnings is, in reality, a part of its "invested capital."

Disclosures About Corporate Liquidity

Will the corporation be able to meet its obligations when they mature? From existing resources? From the cash results of near-term operations? Only with further financing? If further financing is required, will it be available? Obviously, the annual report to stockholders cannot answer definitively these questions about the future. Often, no one can with any degree of assurance. Although the critical near-term may be viewed with some degree of clarity, the longer into the future the maturity of obligations, the more meeting them depends upon results from *future* operations of the corporation than upon present financial condition. Moreover, for corporations pressing their financing limits, the attitude of external suppliers of credit and capital will be a controlling factor—something an annual report cannot be expected to reveal.

However, there is considerable disclosure in the annual report to stockholders bearing upon the corporation's known present liabilities, commitments, contingencies, and liquid assets. This will be found in the balance sheet, footnotes, supplementary information, and management's commentary.

In the balance sheet, cash, marketable securities, and receivables are, of course, the assets most pertinent to the corporation's ability to meet near-term obligations. Sale of securities and collection of receivables are the only steps remaining to obtain the cash to make payments. Market-price valuations of securities and reserves for uncollectible receivables are usually disclosed to reach even closer toward the estimated cash-equivalent.

Inventories, prepaid assets, and deferred charges are in a different category, since they are deferred costs carried forward to be offset against *future* revenues. Thus, their realization depends largely on the adequacy of the latter. They are normally included in "working capital," however, because they are closely related to amounts of liabilities deducted in arriving at working capital, particularly accounts payable and accrued expenses. This is quite consistent with the assumption of a going concern, the continuity of the usual corporation's operations, and its indefinitely long life.

It should be understood, however, that deferred costs are not intended to be assets-in-liquidation. In that unhappy event, *all* liabilities represent presentations for payment, whereas the deferred costs become assets only to the extent realizable at salvage value or distressed sales. Even a portion of accounts receivable, beyond the provision for uncollectibles on a going-concern basis, may not be realized in forced liquidation. As any experienced banker will testify, many a debtor near the financial brink has recovered with guidance and the necessary patience from his creditors. Thus, continuance as a going concern, of itself, is often an asset to the concern involved, as well as to its creditors.

Besides current status of liquid assets and amounts of liabilities due and payable in, say, the next year, information as to the later maturities of fixed obligations is usually disclosed. This may be in the form of dates and amounts of all future maturities, or those in each of the next few years and totals of amounts payable thereafter. This applies to funded debt, lease rentals, and the like. Such disclosures could be highly important to stockholders of corporations near the ragged edge of inability to meet their maturing obligations.

An increasingly frequent disclosure in annual reports, and

one to be commended, is a statement showing the source and application of funds. This is an analysis derived from the income statement and balance sheet, designed to give a concise summary of major sources and dispositions of working capital (in some statements, cash itself). It deals with the outflow as well as the inflow of funds and, for this reason, is much more balanced and less likely to be misleading than statistics with some such title as "cash flow" or "cash earnings." The latter deal only with cash *in*flow from operations (i.e., net income before deducting depreciation and other important noncash costs) which may be more than offset by the year's cash *out*flow for items that will be costs in future income statements. Cash flow statistics have all the deficiencies described earlier for the cash basis of accounting, plus the added one of being incomplete even under that standard; they can be misleading in unsophisticated hands.

Disclosures are customarily made of important events occurring after the date of the financial statements but before issuance of the annual report. Many have an important bearing on future corporate liquidity.[2]

Disclosures bearing upon corporate liquidity in corporate financial reports to stockholders are not designed for the creditor —particularly the short-term lender such as the commercial banker. He may well need many additional pages of analyses and commentary, the inclusion of which in reports to stockholders would decrease understandability for most, and might also put the corporation at competitive disadvantage. However, the banker is in direct, private contact with the corporation and thus can specify and receive information directed at his specific requirements.

---

2. *Accounting Trends & Techniques* (1964 ed., p. 147) reports that in 1963, 176 of 600 companies reported 231 post-balance-sheet events. Most of these had implications of cash inflow or outflow.

Historical Summaries

The point has been made many times that one year is an extremely short segment of time for which to measure the continuous, often long-cycle operations of most corporations. This means that the longer the period, the more reliable the measure of corporate progress. Most conventional financial statements in reports to stockholders are now given in comparison with the preceding year. Thus, two years are covered. Prospectuses issued under the Securities Act of 1933 usually have the closing balance sheet and statements of income and retained earnings for three years, and a summary of earnings covering five or more years.

However, the greatest acknowledgment of the usefulness of historical data over a long period of time is represented by the historical summaries included in annual reports to stockholders. That these purely voluntary disclosures by managements, beyond any externally imposed requirements, have become established practice is indicated by the fact that 81 out of the hundred large industrial corporations furnished historical summaries, as follows:

NUMBER OF YEARS COVERED	NUMBER OF COMPANIES
4-9	18
10	52
11-20	6
Over 20	5
	81

These summaries ranged in coverage from rather complete data to a few highlights from balance sheets and income statements. The important figure of net income is invariably included. Not so frequently stated are the unusual charges and credits reported outside the net income figure.

One of the most important opportunities for improvement in

financial reporting is for all corporations to join the pacesetters in such disclosures or, better yet, to become pacesetters themselves. Further improvements can result from a crystallization of thought as to the type and form of information that can be most useful. In this connection, these recommendations for the future are offered:

1. The historical summaries should cover at least ten years. The feasibility of this has already been established for large corporations. Ten years is long enough in most cases to cover cycles deriving from both external and internal factors and to demonstrate frequency and magnitude of unusual adjustments.

2. At least the significant subtotals from balance sheets and income and retained earnings statements should be included, as well as useful quantity statistics. Useful per-share statistics should be furnished.

3. Unusual charges and credits should be reported immediately after the amount of net operating income for the year, and the net or total amount of the two should be obtained. This should be done whether the items were originally reported as "special items" or as adjustments of retained earnings. As a general rule, the results of unusual transactions and events should be included in the year they were originally reported, rather than thrown back to the years to which hindsight shows that they were more directly applicable. This is recommended because, in evaluating the significance of current results and particularly of current unusual items, it is important to know the frequency, size, and direction of such items in the past. However, if the unusual charge or credit arises from a change to an accounting method that would also have been acceptable in prior years, consideration should be given to adjusting prior years' results for the change.

4. After a merger or acquisition of a business, careful consideration should be given to revising the corporation's previously reported data to include data for the merged or acquired business. The objective is to make trends in historical data after mergers and acquisitions comparable with earlier data. It is recognized that objections can be raised to *pro forma* data for what were formerly separate enterprises and that often rather important judgments must be made as to how this is done. However, in terms of usefulness of information to stockholders, the objections are often greater to historical summaries inflated in the latter years by acquired businesses so as not to be comparable with the earlier ones.

The advisability of immediate write-off of goodwill attributable to a purchase of future earnings was discussed in the previous chapter. Arguments for setting up an amount for goodwill in the balance sheet and then amortizing it by charges against net income would be weakened considerably if the historical earnings were adjusted so as to be comparable with those of the enterprise as now enlarged.

It is easier to avoid establishing an amount for goodwill, and to adjust historical data on a *pro forma* basis, when an acquisition is for stock rather than for cash. Retroactive per-share data can also usually be derived. Where cash is the consideration given, the additional assumptions required to combine businesses on a retroactive basis may be so debatable that the usefulness of the historical record produced would be dubious. Instead, the inclusion in the ten-year summary of a charge for immediate write-off of the goodwill may be the more useful disclosure. However, restatement of prior years' data in historical summaries for some acquisitions for cash deserves experimentation.

The evolution by managements of the long-term historical summary is one of the most important improvements in corporate financial reporting in recent times. Such a summary recognizes and compensates for the fallibility of single-year statistics and is entirely consonant with the long-term and continuous nature of corporate operations. With appropriate recognition of the need to distinguish between the results of current performance and the occasional unusual adjustments, and of the value of adjusting data in connection with mergers and acquisitions, the historical summary could easily become the most useful single statement presented to stockholders. Commentary by management on the cause and significance of fluctuations in important items in the ten-year summary could make it even more significant.

Supplements to Annual Reports
to Stockholders

During the preceding discussion, there have been many suggestions for additional disclosures in corporate financial reports. Virtually all of the recommendations have precedents. Those experienced in preparing corporate financial reports may, however, have envisioned a resulting document as voluminous, technical, and hard-to-comprehend as the early registration statements under the 1933 Securities Act.

Many stockholders are unable or unwilling to digest a communication of financial data beyond a relatively low degree of complexity. The corporate financial report must bear them in mind. Accordingly, it should not be made overly complicated.

On the other hand, there is a growing body of sophisticated investors and analysts (the "institutional" investors themselves constituting a significant group) who *can* digest the more comprehensive and detailed disclosures. They are demanding more financial information about the corporation, and getting it. To the extent that corporate directors, officials, and employees make disclosures to them—wittingly or unwittingly—that are not made simultaneously to the remaining stockholders, the corporation runs "insider information" risks.

The solution would seem to be along the lines already developed by a small number of corporations: an annual report sent to all stockholders which remains a simple document comprehensible to the relatively unsophisticated, and a supplementary report, available on request and so stated in the annual report. In the latter, any limitations on disclosure arising from assumptions as to lack of sophistication among the readers would be abandoned. Corporate secrets, the disclosure of which would ultimately be detrimental to the stockholders, would not be included, of course. Short of that, the scope of the supplemental report would be defined only by the limits of what corporation officials would be willing to disclose privately to analysts and other representatives of institutional investors.

The supplementary financial report for the sophisticated investor has already been invented and developed. It is a communication vehicle of the future for the corporation.

SUMMARY

Notwithstanding the very considerable disclosure that is currently to be found in corporate annual reports, it is in this area that perhaps the greatest opportunity for improvement lies. Whereas precedent can be found for almost any item of desirable disclosure, in general, disclosure practices are uneven. It would also be particularly useful to stockholders to have some insight into the reasoning behind some of the judgments exercised by managements in preparing and presenting financial reports.

In historical summaries, a large number of corporations have gone considerably beyond any minimums suggested or prescribed by external authorities. In doing so, they have seized upon a communication vehicle that is consistent with the nature of the large corporation and useful to its stockholders. Some refinements are needed in many present historical summaries, but this document has the potential of becoming the most useful statement included in the annual report.

The supplement to the regular annual report is the logical answer to the additional informational needs of the more sophisticated investors. It is to be encouraged; the future will undoubtedly see it used more extensively.

VIII
Those Responsible for Financial Reports

Corporate financial reports are produced by people. Who are they? If a number of different people influence the estimates and judgments behind the reports, what are their several responsibilities and authorities? What should they be, under our social system? Responsibility and authority for corporate financial reports is decentralized at the present time. Nonetheless, there are checks and balances that provide for both assignment of responsibility for transgressions and opportunity for innovation as conditions change.

In the discussion of corporate financial accounting and reporting up to now, reference has hardly been made to accountants. This has been intentional—to counteract an imbalance. Corporate financial reporting seems to be considered by many to be the private domain of accountants as a group and of independent public accountants in particular. That this is erroneous is demonstrated by the extent to which corporate financial accounting and reporting can be discussed with reference to the corporation, its activities and its environment, and without reference to accounting theories that may be mysterious to many.

There are, in actuality, at least these parties at interest and with influence on corporate financial accounting and reporting: the stockholder (and his advisers); management, including the Board of Directors; the independent CPAs; the Accounting Principles Board of the American Institute of Certified Public Accountants, the national professional organization of CPAs; the stock exchanges, principally the New York Stock Exchange; and the Securities and Exchange Commission.[1] There follows a brief discussion of the responsibility lodged with each of these groups, the authority each has to carry out its responsibility, and its accountability for these functions.

STOCKHOLDERS AND THEIR ADVISORS

Stockholders and their advisers have, directly, neither responsibility nor authority in connection with the *preparation* of corporate financial reports. If particular stockholders have need for information they are not receiving and have the opportunity to make their wants known, they undoubtedly have a responsibility to do so. After they have done this, management must consider whether it is feasible to accumulate and supply the information and whether the furnishing is in the best interests of all the stockholders.

Stockholders and their advisers have responsibilities as *users* of the communication, however. They must use due care and diligence in digesting the information that they receive. For example, any investment decision made solely upon the basis of such a simple statistic as earnings per share does not conform to the stockholders' responsibilities and no one should be accountable to him for any damage he incurs as a result.

As discussed in Chapter III, it is a function of analysts and investment advisers, as well as sophisticated investors, to make comparisons among companies in connection with investment

---

1. There are also regulatory and supervisory agencies having authorities, responsibilities, and influences in connection with specific industries. These were referred to in Chapter IV and are excluded from the discussion here, which deals with the more pervading influences. The impact of the courts is excluded for the same reason; their influence to date has been centered largely on issues arising out of regulatory—particularly, rate-making—processes and income taxation.

recommendations and decisions. Occasionally, one hears remarks from some of these groups to the effect that each corporation's financial report should be prepared in such fashion as to be automatically comparable with all others. The selection of accounting practices is only one aspect of the role of judgment and estimate entering into the preparation of financial statements. Responsible managements and CPAs agree that cooperation to eliminate differing practices not justified by differing circumstances is a worthy undertaking. However, managements and CPAs alike should not give the impression that they assume a responsibility for accomplishing what they cannot accomplish—absolute and automatic comparability among corporate financial statements. These points should be stressed:

1. Financial reports reflect facts, judgments, and estimates. The latter two will be affected somewhat by programs, policies, and temperaments. No one corporation can synchronize itself in such matters with all other corporations, nor can any external body do the job for all, no matter what its authority.

2. The corporation discloses, in addition to the results of facts, judgments, and estimates, many of the means of arriving at them (such as important accounting practices, unusual charges and credits, and contingencies). If more of such information is needed, it should be requested. In this connection, the usefulness of well-prepared historical summaries covering ten years or more could well be emphasized.

3. The making of comparisons for investment purposes is essentially the function of the analyst, not of a management or its CPAs. In fact, *differentiation* among corporations is a key instrument in making an investment decision.

That corporate managements and their independent accountants should take every opportunity to make financial reports more useful to investors and their advisers seems quite clear. That responsibilities properly belonging to investors and their advisers should not be assumed by managements and their accountants seems equally clear.

MANAGEMENT, INCLUDING THE BOARD OF DIRECTORS

Under our economic system, the Board of Directors of a corporation has the responsibility to render an accounting of its stewardship, which includes financial reporting, to the stockholders. In practice, the directors delegate most of the details of preparing the financial reports to management, and usually not all these members of management are directors. Nevertheless, it is the directors who take the ultimate responsibility for the end product.

In most corporations, the directors and management take the prudent step of seeing that independent CPAs are retained (the exceptions in large corporations being in the railroad, insurance, and banking fields, and these exceptions are decreasing in number). They then rely heavily on the advice and opinion of these experts in the field of corporate financial reporting and thus, properly, transfer some of their responsibility to them. The transfer is by no means complete, however. A member of management or the board cannot transfer primary responsibility even though the independent accountant has agreed with management's financial presentation.[2]

Management has great responsibility for the form and content of the corporation report, including financial statements; it also has commensurate authority to discharge that responsibility. Many laymen assume that a corporation's financial statements have been "prepared" by the certifying CPA. That is not true. The independent accountant may have been highly persuasive in

---

2. The fundamental and primary responsibility for the accuracy of information filed with the Securities and Exchange Commission and disseminated among the investors rests upon management. Management does not discharge its obligations in this respect by the employment of independent public accountants, however reputable. Accountants' certificates are required not as a substitute for management's accounting of its stewardship, but as a check upon that accounting.
—In the matter of Interstate Hosiery
Mills, Inc., 4 SEC 721 (1939)

arriving at figures and words, but ultimately the only thing in the annual report which the certifying CPA owns is his opinion. All else belongs to management. The latter may—in financial statements, footnotes, supplementary tables, and commentary— call "black" what the certifying CPA thinks is "white," and all that the certifying CPA can do about this is to state what he thinks in his opinion. Such confrontations are not typical, of course, because most differences between managements and certifying CPAs are resolved before the financial report is published. Nonetheless, it is a fact that management's authority with respect to the form and content of the corporate annual report is final, commensurate with its heavy responsibilities.

Management, including the directors, is accountable for the authority it has and exercises. If its authority is used imprudently to the end that stockholders suffer damage from false and misleading reports, management may be liable. This is as it should be under our economic system. Any suggestions that management be forced, against its will, to accept a judgmental decision arrived at by an external party, be it the selection of an accounting practice or otherwise, should be considered in the light of the responsibility-authority-accountability interrelationship. Management cannot be relieved of the second, and left with the first and third. On the other hand, if management is *persuaded,* through its own judgment, that an external consensus also discharges its responsibilities, there is no problem. This is usually the way it works. There is an interplay of forces and ideas, rather than unilateral decision by external authority.

Instances can be cited in which managements have been less than forthright in the fullness and fairness of their financial disclosures to stockholders. These practices are to be deprecated not only by parties directly affected, but also by all those interested in preserving the health of the corporate enterprise system. The sad stories are, in fact, relatively few for the larger, publicly owned corporations. They are more than offset by the instances in which managements voluntarily jump ahead of minimum requirements in useful disclosures.

Corporate financial reporting in the United States certainly equals, if it does not exceed, that anywhere else in the world. This position did not come about through a set of centrally created rules; it resulted mostly from a multitude of individual corporate attempts to provide useful financial reports. As long as corporate managements are made to feel that corporate financial reporting continues to be one of their responsibilities, progress should continue. If ever they should be convinced that the responsibility has been assumed by some external body, stagnation in corporate financial reporting would be in prospect. The consistent improvement in the skill, competence, and perspective of corporate financial executives which has been witnessed in recent decades indicates that corporations continue to equip themselves to discharge their share of the responsibility for financial reporting.

THE INDEPENDENT CPA

The independent CPA whose opinion is attached to a corporation's financial statements has the responsibilities of an expert. He is responsible for possessing at least the minimum competence and skills called for in the profession, for using due care, and for formulating professional judgments only upon proper foundations. His responsibilities are not general, but run to the specific financial data to which his opinion is attached. In that opinion, he must pass professional judgment upon: (1) the broad measurement guidelines invoked; (2) the accounting practices resulting from application of the guidelines to particular facts and circumstances; and (3) the fairness of the results produced. The third is the most significant, since it is the ultimate test (it is the *only* test in some other countries).

The independent CPA also has a responsibility to participate with others in the professional, business, and financial communities in formulating and articulating guidelines for measuring financial data. These guidelines are few in number and capable of very widespread application. He also should assist in narrowing the range of accounting practices where it is feasible to do so, especially in groups of corporations that have similar facts and circumstances for which a given accounting practice would be preferable to others.

The CPA's responsibility runs to passing judgment on the appropriateness of any practice to a particular situation. He is not relieved of this responsibility solely because the practice employed has emerged from an external consensus. On the other hand, if the particular practice employed *departs* from a consensus, the burden is strong on the independent CPA to justify his acceptance of the departure. As a practical matter, most guidelines and practices emerging from a consensus are better, or at least as good, as alternatives when applied to the particular facts and circumstances of a given corporation.

The inherent authority of the CPA over a corporation's financial statements is, technically, nil. All that he owns in the annual report to stockholders is his formal "opinion." However, his advice and recommendations usually carry great weight with his client. The threat of a "qualified opinion" carries tremendous force with the managements of most publicly owned corporations. Thus, the powers of persuasion and influence on a corporation's financial accounting and reporting by its independent CPA are strong—a kind of indirect authority without the power of compulsion. For unregulated corporations, only a stock exchange or the SEC have, by force of contract and law respectively, the power to *force* a corporation against its will to alter its financial accounting and reporting.

Authority or not, CPAs can share in the credit for the advanced state of the art of corporate financial reports. Working individually with their clients, and collectively in their profession, they have an excellent record of viewing broad trends in business and finance and extracting the essence for application in individual corporations.

The accountability of the CPA for the discharge of his responsibility (and the exercise of his authority and influence) is similar to that of any other professional man. By far the greatest price that he pays for poor professional work or judgment is damage to his reputation—in the eyes of his client, the business and financial community, and the public in general.

He has other more precise accountabilities for financial statements regarding which he has given his unqualified opinion. If the statements come under criticism because of management's and directors' estimates or judgments with which the CPA concurred, the CPA has an expert's obligation to defend them. In addition, in the large corporation, where it is not feasible for directors and top management to have personal knowledge of financial position and results throughout the enterprise, the CPA is accountable to them to exercise due care in obtaining specific facts having a material bearing on the financial statements and bringing them to the attention of top management and directors.

In most financial reports to stockholders, the CPA's opinion is directed only to *this year's* financial statements. This is true even though data for at least two years are usually presented in conventional financial statements and data covering many prior years are contained in historical summaries. This concentration of the CPA on the current year would seem to be an anachronism. It would suggest that he has not grasped as much as has management the growing meaningfulness of the historical summary in reports of the large, publicly owned corporation. The CPA's professional skill and competence can be utilized to improve the usefulness of historical summaries. Although he has been consulted informally regarding them by most managements, and in some cases has enlarged his opinion on financial statements to cover them, there seems every good reason why historical summaries should invariably be accompanied by a CPA's opinion as to their fair presentation.

THE ACCOUNTING PRINCIPLES BOARD

The Accounting Principles Board is a creation of the American Institute of Certified Public Accountants. It has been charged by the AICPA (through its governing body, the Council) with researching, formulating, and enunciating the best of accounting thought and with narrowing areas of difference and inconsistency in accounting practice. It is a successor to the AICPA's Committee on Accounting Procedure, which operated for some two decades quite effectively on a smaller scale—particularly in research—than the APB.

The responsibilities of the APB are those lodged with it by the profession, but it has been encouraged to assume and discharge them by both the New York Stock Exchange and the SEC.

The APB discharges its responsibility, for the most part, by the issuance of formal, numbered opinions. The authority attaching to them is succinctly stated in this portion of a standard footnote accompanying all opinions: "The authority of the opinions rests upon their general acceptability." Thus the APB's authority over corporate financial accounting and reporting, like that of practicing CPA's, is more that of the power to influence intellectually rather than the power to command. The standard footnote to APB opinions goes on to say: "While it is recognized that general rules may be subject to exception, the burden of justifying departures from the Board's recommendations must be assumed by those who adopt other practices." The applicability of this sentence to a corporate management is probably only indirect in that an external body passing judgment on a corporation's accounting practices would use an APB opinion as a strong authority, but not necessarily the only one.

The applicability of the quoted caution to the independent CPA is undoubtedly more direct, since the APB is a formally authorized instrument of his professional organization. Since the CPA cannot ignore his personal responsibilities, however, the extent to which an opinion binds him, in reporting on the fairness of a corporation's financial statements, must still turn upon its superiority in comparison with alternatives. A good measure of this is usually suggested to him by the extent to which the APB opinion achieves general acceptability while alternatives do not.

The Council of the AICPA recently adopted the position that, commencing with financial statements for 1966, departures from APB Opinions (and bulletins of the former Committee on Accounting Procedure) must be reported in the opinion of a member unless reported in footnotes to the financial statements. The practical effect of this step remains to be seen. Probably the effect will be felt most by the APB itself, in that it will be more cautious than otherwise in stepping out ahead of current accounting thought and practice in an attempt to set direction and pace. The value of references to departures from APB opinions in the future will, as in the past, depend exclusively upon the wisdom of the opinions and, therefore, their persuasiveness.

As to authority, then, that of the APB stems essentially from its intellectual influence. To the extent that APB opinions are enforced by the stock exchanges or the SEC, this does not result from any inherent authority of the APB but from the fact that its opinions are persuasive to the other two groups. Past experience shows that when all three groups reach agreement on some aspect of financial accounting and reporting, the conclusion rapidly achieves general acceptance.

The accountability of the APB for the discharge of its responsibility and the exercise of its authority and influence is at present much like that of the CPA. Its reputation is at stake. Its stature could be damaged by failure to issue opinions on subjects that need to be covered, as well as by the issuance of opinions that prove to be unwise.

This form of accountability for its actions will probably continue as long as the APB's only authority rests upon the general acceptability of its opinions. If the authority of the APB should become more direct upon either the CPA, in dictation of what should be his professional conclusion, or upon managements, as a dictation of their stewardship judgment, the APB would appear then to become accountable for its actions to the courts.

STOCK EXCHANGES

The role of the stock exchanges in corporate financial accounting and reporting will be discussed here in terms of the New York Stock Exchange. The responsibilities and authorities of the other stock exchanges are the same.

The New York Stock Exchange has the responsibility of any exchange: to standardize to the maximum possible extent the specifications of that which is traded on it, and to see that there is made available to prospective buyers and sellers all available information pertinent to their buy/sell/hold decisions. For the larger corporations, since expectation of near-term liquidation does not exist, it might be said that what is being bought and sold is a call upon future net income.

The focus being on net income, it might be considered the responsibility of the exchange to "firm up specifications" for measuring it. This it should, and has, assisted in doing. To the extent that it is impracticable to write such specifications because of the complexity, judgment, and estimate involved, the next responsibility of the exchange would seem to be full and fair disclosure to seller and buyer of all available and pertinent information. A further responsibility of the exchange would appear to be to dispel misconceptions such as that the progress of a corporation can be measured solely by the single statistic of earnings per share.

The authority of the exchange with respect to the financial reports of corporations listed on it derives from its contract with them. It is in a position to force corporations on its list to adopt its accounting and reporting recommendations, under threat of de-listing. The extent of this force depends upon the value to the corporation and its security holders of having the securities traded on the exchange, and this is substantial. In short, the exchange is in a logical and effective position to enforce on corporations measures designed to improve and to narrow areas of difference in accounting practices.

The accountability of the exchange for its financial accounting and reporting requirements rests, again, essentially upon their general acceptability—their reasonableness. If the exchange should fail to establish necessary minimum requirements, it would come under criticism from the investing community; if the inaction were blatant, loss of confidence in the securities listed on it would undoubtedly ensue. On the other hand, if the exchange's requirements should become unduly burdensome, corporations would no doubt withdraw their securities from the list and new listings would not be forthcoming. It would cease to be a successful institution.

THE SECURITIES AND EXCHANGE COMMISSION

This discussion of the role of the SEC excludes its activities in connection with regulated industries and is confined to those in connection with annual reports under the Securities Exchange Act of 1934.

The key phrase describing the SEC's responsibilities in financial accounting and reporting lies in the introductory words of the 1933 Act: "An Act to provide full and fair disclosure . . ." Elaboration of this theme is to be found in phrases such as this in the 1933 and 1934 Acts:

> The Commission may at any time issue an order preventing or suspending the use of a prospectus . . . if it has reason to believe that such prospectus . . . includes any untrue statement of a material fact or omits to state any material fact required to be stated therein or necessary to make the statements therein, in the light of the circumstances under which such prospectus is or is to be used, not misleading.

The SEC has the authority by law to discharge the foregoing responsibilities, as is indicated by this quotation from Section 19(a) of the 1933 Act (substantially the same as Section 13(b) of the 1934 Act):

> The Commission shall have authority, for the purposes of this title, to prescribe the form or forms in which required information shall be set forth, the items or details to be shown in the balance sheet and earning statement, and the methods to be followed in the preparation of accounts, in the appraisal or valuation of assets and liabilities, in the determination of depreciation and depletion, in the differentiation of recurring and nonrecurring income, in the differentiation of investment and operating income, and in the preparation, where the Commission deems it necessary or desirable, of consolidating balance sheets or income accounts of any person directly or indirectly controlling or controlled by the issuer, or any person under direct or indirect common control with the issuer. . . .

The SEC has carefully and wisely avoided prescribing accounting practices on an across-the-board basis. This seems reasonable and appropriate in relation to its responsibilities, for any prescribed detail approaching a chart-of-accounts basis would give it some measure of responsibility for the resulting figures. The SEC's basic approach has been to accept any accounting method which has "substantial authoritative support." In this connection, it has given very strong support to pronouncements of the AICPA and to positions of the independent certifying accountants where either approval or disapproval of a corporation's practices has been involved. This approach has made it the most successful of the federal government's administrative agencies in the field of financial accounting and reporting.

The SEC may, at a glance, appear to be in much the same position as other federal agencies that *do* prescribe accounting rules in terms of detailed charts of accounts, such as the Interstate Commerce Commission, Federal Power Commission, and Civil Aeronautics Board. However, there are these important differences: (1) the others are dealing with *relatively* homogeneous units in particular industries—SEC deals with heterogeneity in its ultimate; (2) the others have rate-making and/or other responsibilities with regard to the economic health of the industry—SEC for most of its registrants has only the responsibility for full and fair disclosure of pertinent information to the investor and, having seen that this is done, takes *no* responsibility for the wisdom of issuing or buying the securities. If the law required it to do otherwise, there could be substantial interference in the flow of capital required for the existence of an investor-owned competitive enterprise system.

Where SEC does exercise the authority vested in it by law to impose financial accounting and reporting requirements upon a registrant, its accountability for the use of sound judgment in the public interest, upon appropriate legal action by the registrant, is to the courts.

SUMMARY

The foregoing presents a picture of a balanced assignment of responsibilities and authorities in connection with corporate financial accounting and reporting. There are checks and balances, but given the particular situation, the assessment of responsibilities can be made. The system accommodates itself to change. In contrast with the rigidity of centrally prescribed, detailed rules, it gives maximum scope for innovation. It decentralizes responsibility and authority to the specific reporting corporation and its independent CPAs. It uses the common rather than the statutory law approach to financial accounting and reporting, in that it emphasizes the facts and circumstances in the particular case; it gives less emphasis to theoretical logic and to centrally made assumptions as to facts. This all seems most appropriate in view of the nature of the corporation, the variety of corporations and the external forces and influences bearing upon each, and the extent to which judgment and estimate enter into corporate financial accounting and reporting.

IX
Equipping for Change

Decentralization of responsibility and authority for corporate financial accounting and reporting must continue, but those who are decision-makers in this subject area should have the guidance of consensuses. The corporation is neither simple nor static. Therefore, full and fair disclosure as to important facts and judgments remains the principal safeguard of both stockholders and managements—indeed, of society. At the same time, it provides the latitude for the innovations that are imperative under conditions of continual change.

The large, publicly owned corporation has, during this century, made an enormous contribution to economic progress in this country as well as in many other parts of the world. It has been able to attract from a multitude of sources huge amounts of capital that it has usually employed profitably. Its relations with stockholders are healthy. Notwithstanding the occasional criticism, it enjoys a high degree of confidence from society at large.

This generally satisfactory corporation-stockholder-society relationship could have been different, and could be different in the future. The aggregation of resources that corporations have the responsibility for developing and over which they have authority is such that the corporation is fair game at all times for social critics. That currently the voices of such critics are relatively quiet can be attributed in some measure, possibly a considerable one, to the high level of corporate financial reporting in the United States. Looking to the future, the challenge is to so adapt financial reporting to changing needs and conditions that it continues to be a pillar of strength in the corporation-stockholder-society relationship.

There are possibly two organizational approaches to further progress in corporate financial accounting and reporting. One approach would move toward concentrating considerable authority in a centralized body for deciding what accounting treatments and reporting practices corporations should use. The other approach would put centralized guidance in the form of advisory opinions, the authority of which would rest upon persuasiveness rather than compulsion but would stress the responsibilities of those who prepare financial reports. Both approaches would focus particularly on eliminating unjustifiable differences in financial accounting and reporting among corporations. There would, of course, be varying judgments as to which differences are unjustifiable.

A choice between these two approaches probably rests more than anything else on the question of whether a method that attempts to achieve a quick solution to short-term problems might create new and serious problems for the longer term. If quick elimination of divergencies among corporations in their accounting and reporting were considered an urgent problem, the solution would require the application to all corporations of a single, strong external force. In our society this could be supplied only by the federal government. Whether or not this would be a feasible solution of the near-term problem in the first place, the question would then arise of whether the federal government could thereafter change its uniform rules as fast as changes occurred in corporations and their environment.[1]

---

1. The same question would apply to any other centralized group which had taken on regulatory characteristics, including the Accounting Principles Board of the American Institute of Certified Public Accountants. The federal government is used in the illustration because only it has the legal authority (subject to restrictions by the courts) to *force* its decisions on the large, publicly owned corporation.

It seems eminently clear that it is not in the nature of the corporation nor its environment that corporate financial accounting and reporting could continue to fulfill successfully its important mission under any form of centralized regulation. On the contrary, the social mechanism that would assure sound adaptations to change as they are needed must have these three components: decentralization of responsibility; the formulation of consensuses; and consistent adherence to the principle of full and fair disclosure.

DECENTRALIZATION OF RESPONSIBILITY

The long-standing decentralization of responsibility to corporate management and directors for full and fair financial accounting and reporting provides the greatest assurance, as compared with any alternative course, that changes to meet new conditions will be made. This direct responsibility to arrive at financial statements that fairly present the financial position and results of operations is quite different from a responsibility to see that the statements do not violate any of an externally prescribed set of rules. In the latter case, attention quite naturally would become centered on the rules and probably on cleverness in finding loopholes. This is a far cry from a *personal* responsibility to arrive at fair financial statements.

Moreover, this personal responsibility should continue to apply, as it does now, to *current* circumstances, which may well have changed from those that existed as recently as a few months ago. In contrast, centralized regulatory bodies cannot respond so readily to change. Where they are dealing with a wide variety of facts and circumstances, it is difficult for them to take a position. And having taken a position, any change is probably harder to make than the taking of the original position. The change must be made for all at once (regulation abhors diversity as nature abhors a vacuum). Thus changing conditions must have rendered the old position clearly outmoded before it is altered, which means that the accommodation comes late, if at all.

There seems little doubt that the assignment of responsibility for the corporate financial report to management and their certifying CPAs provides the mechanism for meeting change better than would a centralized authority.

THE FORMULATION OF CONSENSUS

When the large number and wide variety of corporations are considered, the strong case for decentralization of responsibility may suggest a picture of uncoordinated chaos. Such decentralization may also seem particularly unhelpful to sophisticated investors and analysts in making comparisons of financial position and results among corporations.

However, there is more coordination than appears on the surface. In the first place, "what others do" is a potent influence on the decision of any corporation as to what it will do in accounting and reporting. Beyond this, however, there are deliberate attempts by industrial associations, the Accounting Principles Board, the New York Stock Exchange, and occasionally the Securities and Exchange Commission, to establish a consensus as to the preferred accounting or reporting treatment in a given situation. These endeavors have been quite successful.

Efforts like the foregoing are constructive and are to be strongly encouraged. Nevertheless, the necessity that corporate financial accounting and reporting be sufficiently unrestricted to respond readily to change should continually be kept in mind. This means, in essence, that any centrally established consensus must be offered as persuasive, not compulsory. If the consensus is sound, it will usually drive out contradictory practices. If it does not fit a minority of facts and circumstances, the burden of justification can be sustained for departures; the same is true if conditions change to those not contemplated in the original consensus. But advancing such a consensus in a way designed to make it compulsory for either managements or certifying CPAs would be to attempt a form of regulation the disadvantages of which have just been discussed. An appropriate, if delicate, balance between the advantages and disadvantages of decentralized responsibility and of the centralized consensus is to advance the latter as persuasive rather than compulsory.

FULL AND FAIR DISCLOSURE

No matter how extensively consensuses on accounting and reporting practices are established and how closely they are followed, the principle of full and fair disclosure must remain the keystone of successful corporation-stockholder and corporation-society relations. No matter how clear and complete are the balance sheet and statement of income and retained earnings, nor how comparable among companies the practices used in preparing them, the information in these conventional financial statements invariably needs to be supplemented. The corporation is too complex to be compressed completely into such confines. Estimates, judgments, and contingencies cannot be reduced to penny-accurate amounts. It is hoped that enough specific subjects for supplementary disclosure have been mentioned to demonstrate this.

Beyond that, however, full and fair disclosure permits safe experimentation which, in turn, makes for maximum progress in financial accounting and reporting. At any one time, some corporations may be expected to be changing from fringe accounting and reporting practices and moving toward an established consensus. Where this is the case, controlling facts and circumstances

on a given subject have probably stabilized to the point where
one, or a very few, practices will serve well in all situations. At
the same time, some corporations should be breaking away from
the established consensus and entering new ground where
changes in practices are required to meet their changed circumstances. Corporate financial reporting must be continually up-
dated and refreshed through innovations in this fashion. The
greatest progress of this type is likely to spring from the individual efforts of corporations and their independent CPAs, because
centralized consensuses tend to follow rather than lead and often
to express the lowest common denominator.

At the same time that an atmosphere conducive to innovation
is provided by decentralized responsibility, investors and analysts
making comparative studies of corporations must be remembered. Full and fair disclosure is the essential bridge between
these two important but divergent pressures.

Summary

Corporate financial reporting has served—and served well—an
important role in preserving a healthy relationship among the
corporation, its stockholders, and the remainder of society. The
deeply imbedded principle of full and fair disclosure has been
embraced by most corporations to the point where their annual
reports to stockholders carry more information than is prescribed
by any external consensus or authority.

The continued decentralization to managements and their
certifying CPAs of the responsibility for application of the principle of full and fair disclosure in specific circumstances, while
providing for the formulation of consensuses to assist them, will
best enable those concerned with the preparation of corporate
financial reports to meet and adjust to the changes of the future

as they occur. This mechanism provides the greatest promise that corporate financial reporting will continue to make its contribution to the corporation's significant role in economic progress in the future.

Appendix

100 Large Industrial Corporations
Composite Statement of Income and Retained Earnings

	MILLIONS OF DOLLARS	
	1963	1962
Revenues:		
Sales and other operating revenues	$66,238	$62,935
Dividends, interest, and other income	1,034	939
	$67,272	$63,874
Expenses:		
Cost of goods sold and operating expenses	$55,466	$53,201
Depreciation, depletion, and amortization	3,563	3,380
Interest	381	377
Provision for income taxes	3,153	2,736
	$62,563	$59,694
NET INCOME FOR THE YEAR	$ 4,709	$ 4,180
Unusual charges and credits (net charge)	19	21
Net income, less unusual charges	$ 4,690	$ 4,159
Cash dividends paid	2,590	2,656
Addition to retained earnings	$ 2,100	$ 1,503
Retained earnings at beginning of year	24,702	23,163
Accumulated earnings of companies brought into consolidation	24	173
Transfer to capital for stock dividends	(226)	(10)
Extraordinary dividend in kind	—	(163)
Extraordinary (charges) and credits	(19)	36
Retained earnings at end of year	$26,581	$24,702

205

100 Large Industrial Corporations
Composite Statement of Financial Position

	MILLIONS OF DOLLARS	
	1963	*1962*
Current assets:		
Cash	$ 2,495	$ 2,542
Marketable securities	5,458	4,800
Notes and accounts receivable	8,419	7,619
Inventories	9,554	9,237
Prepaid expenses	225	215
	$26,151	$24,413
Less—Current liabilities	10,136	9,203
Working capital	$16,015	$15,210
Long-term investments and receivables		
Subsidiaries not consolidated	$ 2,807	$ 2,869
Affiliates	243	254
Other receivables	490	472
	$ 3,540	$ 3,595
Property, plant and equipment		
Cost	$65,252	$61,487
Less—Accumulated depreciation, depletion and amortization	33,385	30,779
	$31,867	$30,708
Other assets		
Intangible assets	$ 223	$ 213
Deferred charges	230	237
Sundry other assets	886	844
	$ 1,339	$ 1,294
TOTAL	$52,761	$50,807
Deduct—Long-term liabilities and reserves:		
Long-term debt	$ 7,129	$ 7,179
Reserves and deferred credits	1,325	1,293
Deferred income taxes	318	250
Minority interest in subsidiaries	685	678
	$ 9,457	$ 9,400
STOCKHOLDERS' EQUITY	$43,304	$41,407

100 Large Industrial Corporations
Composite Statement of Financial Position (*Cont'd*)

	MILLIONS OF DOLLARS	
	1963	*1962*
Stockholders' equity represented by:		
Preferred stock	$ 1,262	$ 1,285
Common stock	10,479	11,155
Capital surplus	5,198	4,444
Retained earnings	26,581	24,702
	$43,520	$41,586
Less—Treasury stock, at cost	216	179
	$43,304	$41,407

Index

About the Author

Herman W. Bevis is the Senior Partner of Price Waterhouse & Co. and has been engaged in the practice of public accounting for more than thirty years. He is currently a member of the Accounting Principles Board of the American Institute of Certified Public Accountants, having previously served as Chairman of the Committee on Long-Range Objectives, Board of Examiners, Committee on National Defense, and as a member of the Executive Committee of the Commission on Standards of Education and Experience of CPAs.

Mr. Bevis received his B.A. degree from Southwestern University at Memphis, Tennessee, and his M.B.A. degree from the Graduate School of Business Administration, Harvard University. He was consultant-without-compensation on accounting and budgeting to the Assistant Secretary of the Air Force (Financial Management) for six years and to the Assistant Secretary of Defense (Comptroller) for one year. He has written many technical articles for professional publications and frequently addresses business, professional and educational groups in the United States and abroad.

This first publication under the Arkville Press imprint was set on the Linotype in Caledonia, with display in Monotype Bulmer, by Slugs Composition Company, New York. It was printed and bound by The Book Press, Brattleboro, Vermont, on paper supplied by S. D. Warren Paper Company. The book was designed by Sidney Solomon, and the colophon was created by Theodore Roszak.